Lights! Camera! Autism!

USING VIDEO TECHNOLOGY TO ENHANCE LIVES

* * *

Kate McGinnity

Sharon Hammer

Lisa Ladson

Foreword by Paula Kluth

CAMBRIDGE BOOK REVIEW PRESS

Cambridge Book Review Press
310 North Street
Cambridge, Wisconsin 53523
Editor: Bob Wake

Book and cover design by Nancy Zucker

ISBN-10: 0-9660376-7-7
ISBN-13: 978-0-9660376-6-1

Library of Congress Control Number: 2010940656

Lights! Camera! Autism!

I would like to dedicate this book to my beloved mentor and friend Dr. Anne M. Donnellan, for continuing to challenge, instruct and nurture me both professionally and personally. Also, in honor of the extensive breadth of research, inspiration and knowledge you have bestowed on the field of autism. The world of autism is a better place because of your presence in it. —*Kate*

I would like to dedicate this book to all of the individuals on the spectrum that I have had the pleasure of learning from over the past two decades. Thank you for continuing to show me how to look at the world in a different way. —*Sharon*

This book is dedicated to all of my "movie stars." Without your inspiration this book would not have been possible. I am in awe every day of your courage and perseverance. Some say how lucky my "stars" are to have me in their lives, but I would beg to differ. It is I who am lucky to have you in my life each and every day, teaching me life's lessons. For that, I am eternally grateful. —*Lisa*

Acknowledgements

The authors would like to thank the many people with autism in our lives who continue to inspire and instruct our work. We are deeply appreciative of our editor and publisher, Bob Wake, for his patience and attention to detail. We'd like to thank Nancy Zucker, our talented graphic designer for her sense of style.

We'd like to thank those who contributed to this book by allowing us to tell their stories: Justin, Zach, Sam Rogers, David Stowell, Roy Bedward and Jenny Potanos, as the facts of their lives help to ground our ideas in reality. And thank you, too, to those who directly contributed to the final chapter: Katherine Rybak; Kathy Kaebisch and Lisa Hoeme as well as those who contributed to the DVD: Aaron Emory, Nichela Ladson, Connie Sue Prochnow, Angela Norman, Jennifer Latek, Dawn Kruhak, Gabrielle & Grace Shay; Krystal Kudwa; Riley Kinoshita; Amy Anhold, Becky Rychlek, Lisa Wendt, Rhinehart Lintonen, Minty Hinterberg, Christine Russell, Sara Stone, Barb Townsend, "Jack Othello" & Nan Negri; August McGinnity-Wake & Lucas Bielejewski.

Thank you to our readers, who provided much needed feedback and encouragement: Judy Endow, Jane Pribek, Michael Shoultz, and Anne Donnellan. And to Paula Kluth who wrote the stunning foreword of which we can only hope our book will be worthy.

Finally, we would like to thank our spouses and children, Toshi, Riley, Logan, Nichela, Rodney, Augie and Bob, for the constancy of their support as we traveled this road of book publication—for the many neglected meals and lost days and nights.

CONTENTS

ABOUT THE AUTHORS

Kate McGinnity is an experienced classroom teacher and trainer, and a nationally recognized consultant in the field of autism. During her tenure as a teacher, she was recognized as the Wisconsin Teacher of the Year and The National Teacher of the Year by the Autism Society of America. For more than 20 years, Kate has been a primary developer and presenter for the Wisconsin State-Wide Autism Training Project, sponsored by the Wisconsin Department of Public Instruction. Kate co-authored (with Nan Negri) *Walk Awhile in My Autism: A manual of sensitivity presentations to promote understanding of people on the autism spectrum* (CBR Press 2005).

Sharon Hammer is a master's level psychotherapist. She has over 15 years experience working with individuals on the autism spectrum and their families. Sharon has provided services in a variety of settings such as in-home treatment programs, schools and clinics. She is currently employed by Imagine a Child's Capacity (ICC). At ICC, Sharon is an educational and behavioral consultant, providing training and consultation to schools, community members and parents. Sharon is a Board Member of the Autism Society of Wisconsin and is committed to increasing awareness and possibilities throughout the community for individuals on the autism spectrum.

Lisa Ladson is an educational and behavioral consultant, working as an independent contractor for Imagine a Child's Capacity in Madison, Wisconsin. She is a former special educator who has served as a classroom teacher, certified resource teacher and behavior specialist. She has also worked with families through the In-home Autism Waiver Program. Lisa provides consultation for families, school districts and other agencies. She has extensive knowledge and experience in creating innovative intervention programs for students with complex learning challenges, including students on the autism spectrum.

FOREWORD

Writing this foreword was very difficult.

It was not difficult because I don't know how to write one. I have written others.

It was not difficult because I didn't like the book. I love this book!

It was not difficult because I couldn't find the right words to describe my impressions. I have plenty to say.

Writing this foreword was difficult because after every section, I was compelled to set the book down and try one of the many techniques or approaches described before coming back to read more. At first, it was fun and then it became comical. The deadline to submit these 500 words kept coming and going and I could not finish the task simply because I could not get through the pages without taking action. On page 50, I saw an idea for using video as a way to help the person tell his or her life story. I dropped the chapter I was reading, called my friend, and immediately began planning such a video for her son. On page 39, I read about using video as a tool to demonstrate a specific support strategy in pre-service or in-service training. I put down the manuscript and shot off an email to a client of mine about a plan to make a video on positive behavior supports. And, when I read about creating a video to use for comfort (page 52), I began plotting how to assemble a video of different train images for a friend who loves railroads.

Using video in the classroom is not new to me as a teaching or behavior strategy so I was not expecting to be so surprised or taken with the material. I have successfully used video to encourage learners, to help students learn new skills or behaviors, to teach teachers about lesson design, and to illustrate the skills and abilities of individual children. I have to admit, however, I never considered the range of possibilities outlined by the authors of this book. When I got the manuscript, I immediately began writing comments like, "Wow! Great idea," "Right!" and "Try this!" all over the margins.

This book challenged me with its many rich ideas, clear and compelling examples, and positive and ever-encouraging voice. It is not only a user-friendly guide, it is also a call to action. Throughout the book, the authors quietly suggest that we think differently about autism and about support. They also show us how to calm, support, encourage, teach, and challenge students with this one simple tool and they compel us to use it often and widely.

In sum, this book is rare. Working as I have in the field of autism for nearly twenty years, I know that the one thing educators and families want is a resource that is as useful as it is thought-provoking. Look no further. If you are holding *Lights! Camera! Autism!: Using video technology to enhance lives* in your hand, you have found one.

Paula Kluth, Ph.D.
Oak Park, Illinois
December, 2010

* * *

Dr. Paula Kluth is a consultant, teacher, author, advocate, and independent scholar who works with teachers and families to provide inclusive opportunities for students with disabilities and to create more responsive and engaging schooling experiences for all learners. She is the author of *"You're Going to Love This Kid!": Teaching students with autism in the inclusive classroom,* the lead editor of *Access to Academics for All Students: Critical approaches to inclusive curriculum, instruction, and policy,* and the co-author of seven other texts.

CHAPTER ONE

Camera ready

Autism: a description

In the decades since Leo Kanner's groundbreaking 1943 identification of autism as an inability to relate "in the ordinary way to people and situations," there have been a multitude of perspectives and definitions. Sometimes these have been negative and wrongheaded, such as an early theory attributing autistic children's challenges to an uncaring "refrigerator mother" (Bettelheim 1967) and a recent claim that autism "steals the soul from a child ... then, if allowed, relentlessly sucks life's marrow out of the family members, one by one" (McCarthy 2007).

The description of autism that underpins this book is a more optimistic one by Judy Endow, who defines autism as a diverse neurology that provides many gifts, as well as some "lemons" from which lemonade can be made:

> I think of my lemons of autism as the fruit of who I am. I was born wired to fit (or not to fit, depending on your perspective) into this world. I cannot change my internal wiring any more than I can change my genes. I cannot change my lemons anymore than I can change my blue eye color or my attached earlobes.
>
> I have autism.
> I have lemons.
> I choose to learn how to make lemonade. (Endow 2006)

Understanding these "lemons" and, even more importantly, understanding the gifts of autism, is essential when determining how and when to use video technology as a collaborative support for individuals in our lives who have autism.

Lemons

To understand the lemons of autism, we must first appreciate how a person perceives and experiences the world. For that perspective, it seems only reasonable, then, that we look to individuals themselves who have autism. The following quotations provide a window into the variety of movement and sensory inconsistencies that some people with autism report experiencing:

> "I believe that my apraxia involves certain messages being sent to the brain and then, in turn, to different parts of my body. I cannot seem to tell my right from my left although I know my right from my left. I cannot seem to find my mouth upon command. I have trouble finding where my nose is when I am asked. I find that my breath will not come when I am asked to blow or when I am asked to take a deep breath. I am unable to draw through a straw. I have trouble sticking out my tongue. I cannot seem to spit the water out when brushing my teeth. I cannot purse my lips when I want to drink out of a bottle. I don't seem to get the message to wave or to smile when I should be responding to someone or something. My autism seems to be apparent in my random use of my hands and feet. My habit of biting is a symptom of my being nonverbal and is mostly due to frustration." (Charles in Hale and Hale 1999)

> "They asked him to point at his body parts, but the boy could not do it. Not that he was ignorant of the parts of the human body, but he was unable to point and identify them in his own self. Pointing at objects was difficult too, as he pointed only at the letters on the board and could not generalize it with the other things. Then the doctors asked the other way around. They touched his legs and hands and so on. They asked him to point on the board. This he did with ease." (Mukhopadhyay 2000)

> "If I meant to go in one direction, my body headed in the other, my head still turned sometimes in the intended direction as my body walked blind in the compelled direction, off on a track of its own. Sometimes the com-

pulsions screamed too loud for awareness to compete. Sometimes the awareness made me want to cut my arms and legs off, pull my tongue out, and stitch my mouth up. If not for a sense of humor I might have killed my body outright in retaliation, but I couldn't do that properly and completely with intention, except as a replay of someone else. Without choice I had come to do the only real option possible. I convinced myself that compulsions were me and life and normality and that as long as they were roughly functional, I wouldn't fight them too much." (Williams 1996)

"Jim, an individual with autism interviewed by Cesaroni (1990), thinks synchronizing his movements is as difficult as trying to make one's eyes blink at opposing times. It is very difficult and would require immense concentration for what typically is an involuntary movement for the rest of us." (Strandt-Conroy 1999)

"I always needed to be on the move. Even when I was made to sit still on a chair, I had to rock it. If I sat on the floor, I needed to rock myself and suck the roof of my mouth—the rhythm and the movement meant I was alive and kept the music going. I think I believed that if I ended the movement, then that would be the end of me." (Lawson 1998)

"Hopelessly I sit while mom calls me to come. I know what I must do, but often I cannot get up until she says, 'stand up.' The knack of knowing where my body is does not come easy for me. Interestingly, I do not know if I am sitting or standing. I am not aware of my body unless it is touching something... your hand on mine lets me know where my hand is. Jarring my legs by walking tells me I am alive." (Chandima Rajapatirana in Wallis 2006)

Autism and the dynamics of movement

Judy Endow once described her inability to get up from the couch as resulting from a sensation that her legs were coming out of the back of her body (i.e., her buttocks) even though her eyes told her differently (personal conversation 2008). Thus, in order to get up, she was left with the choice of trusting either her eyes or her proprioception (see glossary), as the two sensory systems were, in fact, working in opposition to each other in terms of the messages they were sending to her.

Donnellan and Leary (1995) believe that many of autism's lemons suggest the dynamics of a movement disturbance (difficulty starting, stopping, combining and executing fluid motion). Further, they argue, these symptoms may affect not only motor abilities, but also speech, thoughts, perceptions, and emotions.

While it is tempting to look for a direct link between an individual's movement lemons and a specific environmental or contextual cause, Donnellan, Leary and Robledo (2006) explain that it isn't that straightforward. Instead, they define movement challenges within the dynamic systems model:

> "A common theme that has emerged in the first-hand accounts fits in well with the dynamic systems model. That is, stress and difficulties with sensation and movement are described by labeled people as not necessarily having a cause and effect relationship. They suggest that the relationship would be better described as a causal loop, instead of as linear as 'A causes B' or 'B causes A.' Instead, stress and difficulties with sensation and movement interact dynamically."

Young (2000) also describes these movement differences as being inconsistent across people and contexts and likens them to "ever shifting sands that seem to have an ebb and flow all their own."

There is increasing evidence that these lemons of autism related to movement and sensory issues are neurologically based. Williams, Goldstein and Minshew (2006) arrived at the following conclusion: "Our paper strongly suggests that autism is not primarily a disorder of social interaction, but a global disorder affecting how the brain processes the information it receives—especially when the information becomes complicated."

Why video for people with autism

We know that using video technology makes sense. During the last forty years, it has increasingly been utilized in everyday educational settings and with good reason. A study done by The National Teacher Training Institute in 2003 found that all students learn more when television and video are incorporated into teaching. In their study, the group of students exposed to videos was both more engaged in their learning and retained more information than those students who were taught using methods that did not incorporate the technology. "Television," according to Betts (1983), "is one of the most powerful agents for change, without which, our teaching would be inestimably poorer." So why do we think using video is an especially powerful medium for people on the autism spectrum? At the most basic level, using video technology appeals to their neurology. It is a good match for many of the gifts and challenges that go along with having autism.

Thinking in pictures

It is now widely believed that many individuals on the autism spectrum think in pictures, as Temple Grandin observed in the title to her 1995 book, *Thinking In Pictures: And Other Reports from My Life with Autism*. Dr. Grandin wrote: "I THINK IN PICTURES. Words are like a second language to me. I translate both spoken and written words into full-color movies, complete with sound, which run like a VCR tape in my head." More recently, Dr. Grandin has compared the way her mind functions to the workings of "Google for Images" (2008). She hears a word and instantly pictures pop into her head that display different pictorial representations of that word. An adolescent with Asperger's syndrome once described his eyes as his own personal "superpower." The visual processing strength and style that is often reported suggests that video technology is compatible with the neurology of autism. "If a picture is worth a thousand words," commented Judy Endow (personal communication), "how much is a videotape worth?" For those who process visually, it seems friendly to that style to teach through pictures and, better yet, video technology.

Watching does not need pre-teaching

Browning and White (1986) found that many students with autism demonstrate what they called "television watching skills." They found that these skills do not need to be pre-taught. The majority of the children in their study already possessed the necessary skills to engage in using video technology. The technology may be a way to present and teach new information to learners who have limited access to other means of instruction. Nikopoulos and Keenan (2006) point out that video modeling "can be a useful medium for learners who cannot take advantage of print materials or complex language repertoires." The use of video technology could help us reach learners who have difficulty with more "typical" types of instruction. When speaking specifically about autism, use of this technology might help those learners who have a hard time sitting still, those for whom the sensory aspects of the usual classroom are difficult, and those who are not yet able to process written information, and those who learn better by watching than listening.

More structure and control

Barring unforeseen electronic mishaps, using video technology can be highly predictable and manageable. The person watching the video has control over the speed, repetition, and volume of the viewing. Charlop and Milstein (1989) found that using video technology created opportunities for repeated viewings. This repetition of material was found to be beneficial to autistic individuals. It may well appeal to the aspect of their neurology that seems to crave sameness and has difficulty with change. While watching videos or accessing the Internet, the social aspects of the everyday world are taken away. There are no "surprise" demands placed upon the individual. There are no expectations of engagement. The interaction is purely between the individual and the electronic device, which is more predictable, consistent, and reliable than most human beings will ever be. Video technology allows us to teach without the "distraction of human interaction" (Neumann 2004). These "distractions" can include the daily variance in the way people smell, sound, and make changes in their visual appearance.

Another benefit of using video technology in supporting individuals on the spectrum is that videos have their own built-in borders. The edges of a TV screen, computer monitor or iPad, offer a crystal clear border of where to start and where to stop attending. Unlike the sometimes overwhelming distractedness of "real-life," there is no focal ambiguity; viewers know exactly where their attention should be.

Supporting behavioral change

One of the many ways that visual technology can be used is in supporting behavioral change in individuals with autism. A word of caution is in order, however. Prior to using any collaborative strategy to support behavioral change it is vital to understand how the behavior is serving the person and what the function of the behavior is (Donnellan 1986; Pitonyak 2009). That is, how the individual might be employing a particular behavior as a solution for their neurological difference (i.e., lemon; Endow 2006).

Sam, a young adult, was having difficulty in the community. He was randomly hitting people. In consultation with his therapists, Sam disclosed that he hit others when "pictures got stuck in his head." He then proceeded to draw the pictures. Through more dialogue, it became clear that when a picture was stuck in Sam's head, his ability to process what was going on around him ceased and he became frozen in movement. When he hit someone else's head, it started his own internal pictures flowing. Sam was able to generate several other solutions for getting the pictures in his head to move (e.g., riding a stationary bike; playing video games; watching "Wheel of Fortune"; doing yoga with his videotape of yoga class).

A system was created whereby Sam made two envelopes. The first had the pictures that were getting stuck in his head. Most of these pictures were scenarios from his past in which Sam thought he was doing something socially appropriate but was instead given feedback that he had misstepped. For instance, one scenario that got stuck was of Sam watching a football game with his family. He attempted to helpfully hand something to someone and inadvertently stepped in front of the television screen during a crucial play, whereby several agitated family members told him to move out of the way. The second envelope had pictures of Sam's solutions (other than hitting) to get the pictures in his head flowing again: play video games; watch "Wheel of Fortune"; jump on his trampoline; ride his stationary bike.

Sam and his primary staff made a training video with Sam as the star, to teach the rest of his staff how to use the stuck pictures and solutions envelopes to support him. In this example, video technology played a role in staff training. Visual strategies played a role in supporting Sam. For other individuals, the solutions might be programmed into a handheld electronic device (such as an MP3 player, iPod Touch, or iPad) or might be made into a PowerPoint choice board that could be viewed on a laptop computer or handheld electronic device.

Easing movement challenges

Jeffrey, a high school student, was having difficulty moving throughout the school. His body seemed to "get stuck" at various places in the school. Jeffrey does not have consistent access to words or speech and was not able to provide insight as to what was happening for him when he got stuck. In this case, the team made their "best guess" about what might support Jeffrey. They designed an intervention around the hypothesis and had him approve the strategies before implementing them.

Jeffrey's team used video technology to assist and support him. First, they showed him pictures on his iPod Touch of where he was next going. Then, they made short video clips of another person walking the route. Jeffrey viewed the schedule words/pictures on his iPod Touch and the short video clips prior to leaving for the next class. Oftentimes, that helped Jeffrey to move more fluidly between classes. However, it didn't always work, and sometimes he still got stuck. When this happened, staff would remind Jeffrey he could view the video clip as many times as he needed to, and he often viewed it repeatedly. While he still gets stuck and there are other support strategies in place for him in addition to the one described here, his fluidity of movement between classes has increased with the addition of video technology into his day.

Jeffrey also had some difficulty during summer school. One day, he ran through a particular hallway, out the door and into the swimming pool, which was located in another building. He jumped into the pool fully clothed while young children were swimming. When Jeffrey and his team got together to problem solve around this, they theorized that he might be having difficulty inhibiting his desire to swim and that once he thought about swimming, his movement got stuck in "high gear."

When school opened in the fall, Jeffrey needed to access the same hallway to board his school bus home at the end of the day. His staff and family were concerned that when he entered the hallway from which he had run in the summer (i.e., to board the bus in the fall), his body might be stuck in the behavior of running to the pool and jumping in with his clothes on. Jeffrey's team designed an intervention that included video technology to support this movement-related behavioral difference. They made a video of students walking down the hallway and boarding the bus. The video was loaded onto an iPod Touch, so he could watch it prior to and while walking down the hallway.

Because they weren't certain if the video would work, they first created a storyboard (in this case, still photos of each step) of Jeffrey walking down the hallway and boarding the bus. They then loaded the sequence of photos onto Jeffrey's iPod Touch. Team members also added a reinforcement video (an unrelated video clip that Jeffrey was fond of) at the end of the "teaching portion" of the sequence. They were careful to refrain from mentioning swimming or not swimming, as they didn't want to trigger his swimming thoughts. Through this strategy, he has been able to successfully board the bus without running to the swimming pool.

Modulating emotion

Tony Attwood (2007) suggests that some people with autism experience emotions in an "on or off" fashion rather than the gradation that most "neurotypicals" experience. That is, a person with autism may be either non-affected or full-blown in anger, while someone with typical neurology might experience other levels of anger before exploding. For a student who might be expressing anger in a manner that is hurtful to himself or others, who seems to simply "explode," one could use a video of a barometer which has a 1, 2, 3, 4 and 5 on it, with different words/phrases depicting levels of anger (e.g., slightly irritated, grumpy, out of sorts, mad, angry, incensed, etc.) to teach the student the different levels and ways they might express themselves at each level.

For a number 5, one might add the use of visual technology by making a PowerPoint slide of the barometer and follow each level by a photo or video clip of what the student could do to express their emotion at that level, as well as a menu of helpful strategies that they might use to calm themselves. For instance, level 5 might have the word "incensed" and the video clip that follows the PowerPoint slide might be of a frustration station or angry room, where the student can go to safely express their anger. Frustration stations look different for different students, and usually reflect how the anger is currently being expressed. For one student who kicked when he became angry, a bolster was put in his frustration station, which he could kick, so he could express his anger without hurting himself or others. When he and his team determined he needed something more portable some of the time than the frustration station (which was in his classroom), his team made a video clip of #5 on his anger barometer followed by a menu of what he could do to calm down, which included stamping his foot on the ground.

Assisting physical education

An area that can give some students particular difficulty is physical education. Reasons for this may include: the physical education environment can be noisy; it can have changing rules as units change; sometimes, there is a different combination of students in a gym class; sometimes classes are held inside, sometimes they are outside, and there isn't always a lot of predictability to when this will happen.

One way video technology has been useful in creating more success for students in physical education is to have them use a Flip video or similar handheld device and videotape the first class of physical education for each unit. This serves a couple of purposes: it provides a safe way for the student to learn about the new unit and also allows them to make their own accommodation, as the video clip can be watched repeatedly between physical education classes. One student who used this strategy watched the videos outside of physical education class and made a chart of the necessary equipment, main objectives of each sport or unit, number of students on a team, etc. It was useful for his PE teacher to see the student's work at the end of the semester.

Help with transitions

Transitioning from one activity or environment to another is a source of anguish for many autistic individuals (Kluth 2003; Kluth and Shouse 2009; Kluth and Schwarz 2008; Endow 2006; Hudson and Myles 2007, etc.). Video technology has been helpful for students in foreshadowing and preparing them for upcoming transitions. A video clip or PowerPoint of an upcoming task or environment can be made and shown when the current activity is winding down. Students sometimes watch it only once or twice; other times they may need to watch it repeatedly before the technique works successfully in supporting them through the transition.

Other benefits

Once the initial equipment is purchased, video technology can be a relatively affordable means of supporting individuals with autism. Neumann (2004) reports saving a great deal of money choosing video modeling over an intensive ABA-based program as a means to teach her son new skills.

Another benefit to using this technology is that it seems to assist in the process of generalization (Buggey 2008). In one study, video modeling was shown to be more effective than in-vivo (live) modeling: individuals with access to video models had faster rates of acquisition of new skills than their control group that had access to live models. Further, the video modeling was more effective in promoting generalization (Charlop-Christy, Le and Freeman 2000).

Neumann (2004) believes there are few (if any) limits to what can be taught using video modeling. This was understood—if less easily implemented than today—over forty years ago when Alger (1969) wrote in regards to the therapeutic uses of video: "It would seem then, that the ways in which videotape can be utilized are probably limited only by ingenuity." By using video technology we are acknowledging the strengths that are inherent for many with autism. "The secret of education," Ralph Waldo Emerson famously observed, "lies in respecting the pupil."

Our definition of video

The more we learn about autism, the more we realize that there are amazing tools at our disposal to assist autistic individuals in meeting their full potential. We see video technology as being a rather new, highly exciting, very effective, seemingly limitless way to support individuals.

For the purposes of this book, we are defining video technology as technology that contains pictures that move or change. This includes, but is not limited to: video from cameras, purchased videos made for teaching specific skills, other media such as TV shows or movies, SMART or Promethean Boards, websites, social networking programs, skyping, and computer software such as PowerPoint. Also portable devices that employ and utilize video technology such as the iPod Touch and iPad, as well as MP3 players, Blackberry, iPhone, Smartphone and other cell phones and handheld electronic devices.

The information in *Lights! Camera! Autism!* is not specific to the currently available technology. Our examples are less about the types of technology used and more about the importance of using video technology for people with autism because it is respectful of the way they may experience the world. As a technological society, we continue to witness change to increasingly efficient and elaborate devices at what seems like lightning speed. The key to incorporating technology in support of individuals with autism is sensitivity and respect.

Target audience

Lights! Camera! Autism! is designed to help anyone who is in a position of providing support to an individual on the autism spectrum. This includes, but is not limited to, parents and other family members, teachers, assistants, therapists, service providers, case managers, and autistic individuals themselves.

CHAPTER TWO

The dynamics of video technology

Video modeling

Recent research has shown video modeling to be an effective way to: increase social interactions (Garfinkle and Schwartz 2002); increase spontaneous verbalizations (Charlop and Walsh 1986), enhance generalization of learned material (Carr and Darcy 1990); generalize community skills (Haring et al. 1995); gain functional living skills (Shipley-Benamou, Lutzker and Taubman 2002); teach perspective taking (Charlop-Christy and Daneshvar 2003); teach verbal and motor responses (D'Ateno et al. 2003); promote social interactions and reciprocal play (Nikopoulos and Keenan 2003, 2004a, 2004b); enhance conversational skills (Charlop and Milstein 1989, Sherer et al. 2001); increase play-related concepts (Taylor et al. 1999); and reduce disruptive transition behavior (Schreibman et al. 2000).

Before you use video modeling as a means to teach new behaviors, it might be helpful to take a look at the basics from the "father" of modeling, Albert Bandura. When Bandura conducted his early research on behavioral modeling, he found that there are certain characteristics that make a model effective. He discovered that the "closer" the model being viewed was to the individual doing the viewing, the more effective the modeling (1969, 1997). That is, the most effective models are those that are most similar to the individual. Bandura found that the more he controlled for factors such as gender, age, race, and ability level, the greater the effectiveness of the model. Other research that supports Bandura's early findings showed that when there was a large discrepancy between the observer and the model, it led to failure to acquire new skills (Muzekari and Kamis 1973). In this study, the researchers recommended using models that had similar behaviors and apparent potential as the observer, so that subjects could identify with them on a personal level.

When considering forms of video modeling, video technology allows for exact repetition of the event being captured. It takes away all the subtle and not so subtle differences that occur when working with live or in-vivo models. It may match the neurological make-up of many individuals with autism who benefit from repetition.

Anecdotal evidence seems to show that when using video modeling, it takes relatively few viewings for observers to learn new skills. Neumann (2004) states that her son usually learns novel skills within 5-10 viewings of a new modeling clip. If he has not learned the lesson after these viewings, then she revises the videotape.

Video self-modeling

Video self-modeling (VSM) is a means to educate an individual by viewing themselves on video, with the intention of teaching a novel skill. Buggey (2009) defines VSM as the manipulation of video so that a person is able to watch themselves performing a behavior correctly or at an advanced level. He further states that "by allowing children to act as their own models, we may be able to considerably strengthen the effects that video modeling has on the viewer." There are a number of different reasons why self-modeling is so effective. As stated earlier, Bandura (1969, 1997) found that the models that are the most effective are those that are the most similar to the individual. There could not be more effective models than the individuals themselves. Whenever possible, have the learner model the behavior for themselves. If this is not possible, it is best to have a model that is similar to the learner.

Another reason may have more of a cognitive-behavioral basis in that we can "trick" our minds into believing that we can do something that we can't. Basically, telling ourselves, "I know I can do it, because I saw myself do it already." Fuller and Manning (1973) found that people showed greater signs of physiological arousal when shown their own image on a video recording when compared to watching videos that they were not in. In other words, watching yourself on video clips may actually increase your ability to attend to the video. Wright and Smith (2009) illustrated the fact that video self-modeling may even have an effect on the physiology of the viewer, with findings indicating that individuals who observed a VSM of themselves doing a specific weight-training exercise actually showed a 3% difference in strength development when compared to those that did not watch a video model.

Most of the current research on VSM consists of case studies or relatively small groups of subjects. Despite this, these studies are providing the beginnings of the evidence base to validate its use. The following studies have shown a wide variety of uses for video self-modeling. In the area of communication and verbalization, Wert and Neisworth (2003) found that they could increase spontaneous requesting using VSM. Buggey et al. (1999) found that they were able to teach individuals to respond correctly when asked verbal questions. When examining the research that has been done on increasing social skills, Bellini, Akullian and Hopf (2007) found that they were able to increase social interactions using VSM, and Buggey (2007) found that he was able to increase play skills. VSM has been found to be an effective way to reduce challenging behaviors such as jumping places in line, becoming upset when not getting called on, tantruming, and eating difficult foods (Dowrick and Buggey 2000; Buggey 2007; Buggey 2009). It has been found to be effective in helping individuals make positive behavioral changes in the areas of hyperactivity, aggression, and sexual problems (Dowrick 1983). There are also benefits in using VSM to target academic skills: reading fluency, classroom participation (Buggey 2009), and math skills (Schunk and Hanson 1989).

Feedforward

Feedforward is a very specific type of video self-modeling in which a person is shown a video of themselves displaying skills that they are not yet able to access with independence (Dowrick 1983). Capturing these skills on video, if they are truly skills a person cannot access yet, could be a bit of a challenge. There are a number of different ways that we can film these clips to make them effective feedforward videos.

The first way to consider shooting a video of this type is to film the individual performing the task with hidden prompts. These prompts could be visual supports or actual physical supports. The trick is to angle the camera in such a way that from the perspective of the camera's lens, the individual appears to be completing the action independently. One example where this works well is to teach self-help tasks like hand washing. The individual washes their hands while receiving prompts from the side or underneath. Shoot the video from the opposite side, being careful not to get the physical prompter in the video shot. This method has been highly successful in teaching this self-help skill.

Editing is another way to manipulate the video to show the individual as being able to complete tasks or demonstrate skills that are not yet in their repertoire. Clips can be edited together to make it look like a specific behavior is following another one, even though there may have been some prompting in-between. An example where this could be put to good use would be to show an individual engaging in a stressful situation and then show them engaging in a relaxing activity (e.g., deep breathing) afterwards. This could begin to chain together the stressful event with a calming, new behavior. Buggey (2009) was successful in using this method as a way to assist children in increasing their Mean Length of Utterance (i.e., how many words they were able to string together at a time). He did this by filming the children imitating single word phrases, and then edited them together to make it appear that they were saying longer sentences.

When shooting the video, the filmmaker could also consider using incentives as a possible means to provide extra reinforcement and increase the level of access the individual has to the targeted skill. One could also film for extended periods of time, and "catch" events that occur rarely. This could make it seem that these rare events happen much more often then they really occur. One final way to make feedforward clips is to figure out if the individual is able to access the targeted skills in specific situations (like only at school or only when they are with Dad). The individual is filmed performing the skill and the film is edited to make it appear as if they are accessing the skill in other environments or with other people (Dowrick 1983).

Positive self-review

Using positive self-review (PSR) is another specific type of video self-modeling. Buggey (2009) describes PSR as reinforcing an already known skill to improve performance or fluency. This is the type of VSM that is often used in sports, when athletes will watch videos of themselves performing at the top of their games. They will watch these videos over and over again as a means of increasing and fine-tuning their athletic performances.

There has not been a lot of research done on positive self-review, but given the plethora of accounts by people with autism regarding difficulty in accessing their skills, it only makes sense that this type of video modeling could be useful for individuals on the autism spectrum.

Shooting your own video vs. purchasing videos

When possible, consider shooting your own video models. Using your own video model will allow for more control over: the model used; the display of the targeted skills; the environment in which the skill is being used; the materials which are being used; and the individuals with whom the model has interactions.

However, there are numerous commercial video-modeling products currently available. Before purchasing, keep in mind the basic guidelines for modeling. Look for videos that have individuals as models that closely match your target individual(s) in terms of age, gender, and ability level. Also, consider purchasing videos that illustrate only positive behaviors.

These pre-made videos may be beneficial for those just starting out in the process of video modeling because they show examples of how the technology may be used and may help in the development of new ideas. Commercial videos may also be useful for those who work with groups of individuals on an on-going basis.

Prerequisites for VSM

There are two prerequisites for using video self-modeling (Buggey 2009). The first is that the individual has some self-recognition that they notice themselves either in the mirror, on the video, or on a video recording device (many digital video cameras have a screen that can be flipped around, so that the person being recorded can see themselves). The other prerequisite is that the individual is able to attend to video displays.

Illustrate only positive behaviors

For the majority of individuals it will be important that video modeling illustrates only the positive behaviors, or the behaviors that we are trying to increase. This will be especially true when using video self-modeling. Both Dowrick (1983) and Buggey (2009) concur that viewing negative behaviors can exacerbate the problems. Dowrick describes a strategy employed by B. F. Skinner when he was enlisted to work with baseball coaches to improve batting averages of ballplayers. Skinner advised these coaches against showing their players their own poor strikes. He suggested instead that players be shown video of themselves hitting home runs. Seeing the less effective ball skills, Skinner believed, could have a negative effect on their self-image and self-esteem.

Roy Bedward, an artist and presenter who has autism, explains that when people refer to a particular behavior of his that he is attempting to inhibit, it becomes more difficult for him to inhibit that behavior. Hearing the behavior mentioned makes it almost impossible for him to avoid engaging in it. Similarly, it may be more difficult for an individual to inhibit an undesired behavior they are seeing themselves doing via video modeling.

There may be certain cases or times in which it is appropriate to show the "wrong" behaviors. If so, it must be done with great care and is best if the individual indicates it is helpful to see the negative or wrong behavior. Always use a sustained visual cue to communicate to the individual watching the video that the behavior is "wrong." The red universal symbol for "no" put over the TV screen can illustrate this. Another idea is to have the models from the video wear hats or stickers marked with "no" while they are taping. When using visuals like these to show that something is wrong, the individual needs to understand the visual support indicating that the behavior is incorrect. In the above example it would be necessary that the learner understand the universal symbol for "no."

Not too far ahead

The most effective models are those who are only slightly more advanced than the learner in performance of targeted skills. Models should be no more than a step or two ahead. If the models are too far advanced from the learner, the skills become "unattainable" and the videos lose their effectiveness.

Using chaining

When using video modeling or VSM, it is important to remember basic behavioral support techniques such as chaining (see glossary). Since it is best if the model is only one or two steps ahead of the learner, skills can be linked together using a forward or backwards chain.

Here is an example of using a forward chain for video modeling to teach an individual how to make a peanut butter and jelly sandwich: The first scene in this video model would be the first step in the process (i.e., getting out the peanut butter). An example of using a backward chain for teaching an individual how to tie their shoes: The first clip shown would be the last step (i.e., pulling it tight) and then adding one step at a time backwards until the learner reaches the first step (i.e., crossing the laces).

Viewing consequences of a model's behaviors

Beyond just viewing of the behavior itself, when the observer watches consequences following the behavior, it strengthens or weakens the observer's probability for imitation of that behavior (Ross 1981; Nikopoulos and Keenan 2006). Thus, to increase the effectiveness of the video model, consider showing the model engaging in an activity that the learner finds reinforcing immediately after showing the model engaging in the new skill.

Leaving a "blank"

Leaving a bit of blank screen at the end of a modeling segment may be useful to allow the individual space to apply the new skills into other areas and not just the ones that have been displayed in the video. Thus, it can help increase the generalization of these new skills into more settings or environments. This technique was used in teaching Carrie the new skill of how to order food at a fast food restaurant. In the video, Carrie was filmed ordering food at three different fast food restaurants. She did this with some verbal and visual prompting that was later edited out of the video. After viewing all three of the restaurant models, the video editor put in a blank screen with the words "Any other fast food restaurant" displayed. These words remained on-screen for about fifteen seconds of viewing time. Then the video ended. This way, Carrie, who sometimes had trouble with generalizations of new skills, knew that the skills she was viewing applied not only to the specific three restaurants in the video, but to any fast food restaurant she might encounter in the future. The video was successful. Carrie has been able to demonstrate the "ordering" skill in the restaurants depicted in the video, as well as other restaurants she has since encountered.

Length of video

When shooting videos for modeling or self-modeling, the length of the video is going to depend on the learner's unique personality and learning style. Consider how long a particular learner is able to attend to typical videos. Also examine if the individual is able to sit for great lengths of time or would benefit from some breaks for movement. Finally, the length of the video will obviously be dependent upon what skills are targeted. If it is a simple skill (like returning a wave hello) this may be shorter in length. If it is a more complex skill (e.g., changing a tire) obviously this will be longer in length. Buggey (2009) reports optimal results when the videos are 2-3 minutes in length.

When starting the video modeling process with a new learner, begin with videos that are shorter in length, making them progressively longer over time.

After your video is shot, Neumann (2004) recommends watching the individual as they watch the video. You can make the determination, based upon their facial expressions and body language how long they are able to attend to modeling videos and just how long might be too long.

How many viewings

Individuals that are using video modeling often report quick, if not immediate results. Neumann (2004) reported that her son would gain most new skills after watching the video model five to ten times. If she did not see changes in the target behaviors in five viewings, she would change something about the video. Buggey (2009) reports that "results are seen almost immediately." He concurs that if you are not seeing results after a few showings, consider trying something else.

We have seen behaviors change after showing a video only one time. Other times, it may take more showings. In many cases, if video modeling is going to work for the individual, it will work quickly. This is especially true when this method is compared to other methods of targeting behavior change.

One new video at a time

We strongly recommend only introducing one new video at a time. It is important that the individual have time to observe the video and then rehearse and implement the new behaviors before another video is introduced. This will limit confusion and help to keep the goals around the new skills more clear.

Once a behavior is attained using a video model, it can be put on maintenance and another video can be introduced. While it is not suggested to introduce more than one video at a time, an individual may be watching some videos for maintenance of a skill while a new video is introduced.

When VM and VSM are not working

If video modeling or video self-modeling have not been successful, there could be a number of ways to rectify the situation. First, make sure that you are not going too far ahead with your modeled behavior. Remember that the most successful models are those which are only one or two steps above the individual's current level of ability.

Check to make sure that your learner is able to identify with the model being shown. Again, keep in mind that the learners are most likely to imitate those that are closest to themselves in terms of: gender, age, race, ability (Bandura 1969, 1997). So check your model. Be sure that the individual modeling the skills is someone that the learner can identify with. If you are not using VSM, consider using it.

In one case, video modeling proved to have a powerful yet unintended effect on the individual. For Matt, any time he watched a video of himself performing a daily routine, he refused to complete the routine later within the same day. This refusal only occurred on days when Matt watched the video before he was to perform the task. Matt's team hypothesized that, for Matt, viewing the self-model was so powerful that he believed that he had already completed the task and therefore didn't need to do so again. The solution was to have Matt watch his videos only after the targeted task was completed in his day. This way he was still receiving the benefits of the model, including increasing his speed and independence with the task, but he wasn't "fooled" into believing the task was already completed.

Finally, if not already doing this, consider adding a level of reinforcement to your model. This could be a completely separate video clip, added onto the end of the targeted video, such as a clip from a favorite cartoon. Or, you can provide some reinforcement outside of video viewing, such as a favorite chair to sit in while watching or a special treat after viewing. Finally, you could show the individual in the video clip receiving reinforcement after performing the skill. In this set-up, the individual watching the video does not actually receive the reinforcement. Rather, the viewer observes the model being reinforced and then enjoying the reinforcement.

A high school student with autism was struggling with several daily living skill tasks. When looking at possible strategies to use in eliminating the need for verbal directions in each step of teaching a daily living skill, his teacher decided to try using video modeling. When this strategy did not seem to be effective, his teacher decided to take a step back and use a PowerPoint presentation with all of the individual steps delineated with still pictures. The student watched the

PowerPoint several times a day over a number of weeks. He was attentive to the presentation and it appeared to jumpstart his skill acquisition process. This same procedure was followed to teach other daily living skills and eventually his teacher was able to include video instruction as well.

Preparation video

Preparation videos are videos that are shot with the intention of preparing the individual for an upcoming event. These videos include the sights and sounds that the individual may experience within a new environment or during a new situation. Neumann (2004) had great success in preparing her son for a doctor's visit when she used a videotape of what was going to happen during a doctor appointment to help him prepare. Videos of this type may actually serve to provide some desensitization to the individual. In another example, Neumann (2004) describes how her son became desensitized to having toys bang and crash into each other. Originally, he was unable to tolerate peers in his environment engaging in this behavior. After repeatedly watching the video of a toy train going off its track, he no longer tried to stop his peers from engaging in this "crashing" play.

One first-grade student with autism had difficulty entering and remaining in music class. He would become distressed during the class, and had even begun to run out of the class into the hallway screaming. His team thought that he actually liked music. He hummed or sang the songs from class at different times in the day. He seemed excited when music was on his schedule. It was the team's theory that once he was in music class, he became overwhelmed with the sounds and the movement involved in the class. He was offered noise-reducing headphones or earplugs, but this did not change the behavior. The team then made a video of the music class, which was shown to him in the morning on the days of the week when music class was scheduled. The change was immediate. After viewing the video the first day, he remained in music class the entire time. Within a month, he was attending music without incident every day and singing songs along with the rest of his class.

Another example of video technology being used for desensitization took place within a special education classroom. Zachary is a third-grade student with autism. Whenever someone would attempt to use the microwave in his classroom, he would cover his ears and start screaming. His teachers videotaped the entire sequence of using the microwave. The adult in the video was a preferred teacher for Zachary. Zachary watched the video three times in succession, each time showing less and less anxiety to the process. After the third time watching it, he displayed no sensitivity to the microwave being used in the video. His teacher then attempted to use the microwave in the classroom and Zachary continued working, showing no stress over the microwave being used. (See DVD supplement.)

Staff training video

Staff training videos are videos that are created with the intention of teaching family, friends and staff members new skills. By providing some training to support people and staff members through video, we ensure that all individuals supporting a person with autism are receiving the same information. We can provide them access to observations that they might not otherwise have. It also allows for more flexibility in training, because people do not all have to be in the same place at the same time to receive the same information. This flexibility can end up providing a cost-saving effect as more can be done from home and people do not have to hire substitutes to cover their usual role while they attend staff training.

Specifically related to the area of autism, this video training could include, but certainly is not limited to: providing staff members with information about a specific individual's likes and dislikes; demonstrating specific teaching and support techniques that are useful to the individual; as a way to show different stages in behavior intervention plans; to demonstrate how the individual uses their personal communication system; to demonstrate how to support using specific visual supports; to coordinate support across environments and to depict how teams are defining specific behaviors. (See DVD supplement)

Self-advocacy video

Self-advocacy videos are videos that individuals either create themselves or ask others to create with or for them as a means of sharing information about themselves or their disability. Some individuals with autism can have difficulty with expressive communication, especially when it is about themselves. Thus, these videos provide an important platform. People can say things on the video that they might not be able to say in front of other people. They also have the opportunity to rehearse or script what is being said on the video. In addition to this, for individuals who do not speak, visuals which describe what they want others to know about them and how they want their autism explained to others can be included in their personal self-advocacy video. Some non-speaking people choose to have voice output added to their self-advocacy videos and others choose to add music or other preferred sounds to personalize their video.

Affirmation video

Affirmation videos are videos that provide the viewer with positive information about themselves. Affirmation videos are used to build self-esteem and self-efficacy. They can also be used as a strategy for calming and relaxation. It can be helpful to use them to help balance out the large amounts of negative input, or the input that they are not good enough, or somehow do not measure up, that some people with autism unfortunately receive on a daily basis.

These videos can exist in almost any medium; we often produce affirmation videos using video clips or PowerPoint presentations. Within the affirmation video, the individual will see and/or hear positive things about themselves like: "I am a unique individual," "I am a creative poet" or "I am loved." These words can be paired with music or visuals that are pleasing to the individual.

Skill-teaching video

Skill-teaching videos can be defined as videos that are designed to teach the learner new skills, but use components other then video modeling. These videos may be more like video social stories (Gray 2000). These are video clips that give the individual information about specific situations or events. They may be videos that give the individual directions, such as a new relaxation routine to follow. Skill-teaching videos also may consist of watching videos, again not to gain the skills modeled, but to identify specific components within the scene. For example, one could have someone watch clips from their favorite sitcoms, cartoons or other television clips, intermittently pausing them to have the individual identify emotions, cause and effect relationships, and hidden curriculum items that occur in the clips. By choosing favorite shows, it heightens the motivation to learn information that may not be automatically acquired by the individual.

Sensitivity video

Sensitivity videos can be used as a means to help others understand what it might be like to experience autism. An autistic person might be encouraged to make a video clip of what they would like their classmates, co-workers, or support team to know about how autism uniquely affects them and their experience of the world. These videos can be used to introduce an experiential sensitivity training, which is used to promote compassion and understanding of what it might be like to have autism (McGinnity and Negri 2005). Some individuals prefer to use premade commercial DVDs to introduce sensitivity trainings.

A means to take data

Using video sampling as a means to take data can be a powerful tool in providing both consistency and objective evaluation of intervention techniques. Videos of this type are shot either as a general sample of skill development or as a means to track specific skills. Data taking using video offers many benefits. As pointed out by Summerfield (1983), taking video recordings at regular intervals may help people to notice small improvements "that might otherwise have been overlooked." Noticing these minor improvements can be important to individuals for whom progress is made slowly. It can show us that progress is being made when the day-to-day observations do not seem to illustrate that fact. Video recording also allows viewers to slow down action and interactions. This may allow them to catch small details and possible behavioral triggers that they might otherwise miss.

For those individuals who seem to be affected by the presence of observers in their rooms, using videos can be an easy way to limit the interference between the observers and the person being observed. Using video technology as a means of tracking data allows an increase in the number of people that can unobtrusively view and interpret a given skill or behavior. This increases the number of raters of behaviors, which increases reliability of the data being obtained. Maxwell and Pringle (1983) found that "the ability to replay all or part of a record makes it possible to develop scoring techniques that are highly reliable and to ensure that this is maintained throughout rating procedures."

Amendment of IEPs and treatment plans

Once you have decided that you are going to be using some form of video technology in supporting an individual or in supporting their staff, it will be important to amend plans to include the use of video technology.

Choosing the technology

Determining which type of technology (PowerPoint, Internet, video) will be used depends upon a number of factors. One thing to consider is what skills you are trying to teach. Another consideration is how often the individual will be using the video and the places they will be when they need to access the technology. Finally, consider the ease with which the technology will transfer to other places.

Teach how to use

When determining which form of technology to use, consider that the learner may need to learn how to use the technology before they are able to access it independently. It may be helpful to start by using a type of technology that the learner is already able to access, like a DVD, and build on that by adding additional types of technology over time. Consider using video modeling to teach the steps necessary to access other technology. For example, a video model can be used to teach an individual the way to sign into and access computer programs.

Facilitating vs. forcing

Watching any teaching video should be a positive experience. A practitioner need not feel like they are coercing anyone; it is optimal for the learner to enjoy the experience of watching the video. If an individual demonstrates a lack of interest in this intervention, it may be helpful to build in more reinforcement, interests and/or positive videos.

Incorporating interests

For some individuals, it may be helpful to build reinforcement into the viewing of a video. This can be done by adding things the individual is passionate about at the end of the teaching segment. Or you can build the passions right into the video. Another method is allowing the individual to watch one of their own preferred videos after they view the teaching video.

Affirmations and celebrations

The use of video to teach new skills is more effective if people are not just watching clips about things they need to improve upon. When the "teaching" videos are mixed in with videos of success, celebration, or affirmation, the effectiveness of the teaching videos increases.

Consider if we can interrupt the video

There are some on the autism spectrum who have difficulty when a video is stopped, paused, or otherwise interrupted. It is best to be aware of these preferences before starting to use video technology. It may be important for such individuals to use videos that are shorter in length (so that there is less opportunity for them to be interrupted). Another option for supporting individuals with this difficulty is to shoot videos in chapters or segmented into "stories."

When to review

For videos designed to teach new skills, it is important to review the skills often. Thus, it is recommended that the video be reviewed at least once a day. It is important to review the video at times when the individual is calm and available for learning. Using the videos during times of distress or upset is usually not recommended (unless the video is designed to be used as a method of relaxation or regulation).

If the video is event specific, consider reviewing it more frequently prior to the event taking place. If you are shooting a video about taking turns going down a slide, for example, you may want to show this video right before the child goes outside for recess. If your video is about a change that is designed to assist the individual in managing stress, it will be important to watch this video before, during, and after the individual experiences the stressful event.

Sometimes it is difficult to determine when watching a video is going to fit into a person's day. Neumann (2004) used her son's videos as a "break" from the typical academic activities of the day. This "break" could be especially acceptable when using some of the affirmation and celebration videos mentioned above.

Taking data

Whenever you are using any intervention designed to change behavior, it is important to take data to measure the effectiveness of the intervention. Data should be taken prior to beginning the intervention, so that a baseline can be established. Then, as the intervention begins, compile data to see how it is affecting the behavior.

Remembering function

Video technology is a powerful medium. It is proving to be a highly effective way to support individuals in making changes in their behavior. In the use of such an effective tool, it will always be important to consider that all behaviors serve a function. This should be taken into account before going forward in trying to teach different behaviors. Remember to keep the original function of behaviors in mind when teaching replacement behaviors.

Digital video vs. VHS tape

It is our bias that digital recording devices are the far better choice when shooting videos for teaching purposes. Recording made with digital devices are usually easier to transfer to computers for editing and sharing with others. The editing process itself is far easier using digital recording over VHS tape. The latest technology not only allows for greater ease of editing, but also the flexibility of adding special effects like titles, voice-overs, music, fade-ins and fade-outs and video clips designed for reinforcement. An advantage of using a digital recording device (DRD) is that still pictures can be obtained from within the digital recording that can be made into additional visual supports.

If a VHS recording device is all that is available, that does not need to be an impediment to using video modeling. We have seen many effective videos using video images that were recorded on videotape cassettes. Additionally, keep in mind that cassette recordings can be converted to a digital format, such as a DVD, with little fuss.

Informed consent

It is important to gain informed consent from any individual that may appear in a video recording (not just the target subject, but others that may appear in any of the shots). Individuals need to be informed of what exactly will happen in the course of video recording. They need to know exactly how the recordings will be used. They also need to know how they can withdraw their consent if they change their minds. Finally, individuals need to be informed of how long videos will be kept, how they will be stored, and how they will be erased. A sample consent form is located in the appendix.

When using hidden video cameras

There may be times when it is beneficial to use video cameras that are out of sight of the individuals in the shot. If you are going to be shooting videos using hidden video cameras, ethics dictate that subjects should be shown all recording apparatus prior to the video recording. The people being filmed should know where all of the cameras are located and how they will be activated.

Making your own storyboard

When shooting a video, it is very helpful to write out a script or storyboard the scenes ahead of time. This will allow the set up of props, actors, scenery as well as the plan for the exact shots. Doing this before actually shooting the video allows more freedom while shooting to concentrate on the technical aspects of using the equipment. (See appendix.)

Rehearsal of skills

When shooting a video with "actors" engaging in the action, it may be important to have them rehearse scenes or specific shots beforehand. This will allow them the opportunity to practice movements and lines. Many children really enjoy this process and get into the idea of "making a movie." Sometimes, when shooting videos, we even incorporate the use of a director's slate board clapper as a fun way to mark rehearsal trials and different scenes.

Point of view

It is important to consider the point of view from which the video should be shot. Whose eye does the camera lens represent? There are two perspectives to consider. One is shooting the video from the individual's vantage point. When shooting a video this way, the camera would be placed at the same level as the person's own eyes and shot from where they would see things. This method may be beneficial for shooting things like teaching someone how to tie their shoes or teaching someone to use their locker. Another point of view is from an unseen observer. This is the way that most TV shows are shot. The camera is pointed at the scene and records everything as if viewed from someone not involved in the action. We have found that some people respond significantly better to visuals and videos when shot from their own point of view. Other individuals may respond better to videos shot from the more global perspective. Response to different perspectives may need to be assessed by providing videos for different points of view to ascertain which works best for that person.

Lighting and camera positioning

One of the best things that one can do before getting all the people together to shoot the video is to film a practice run. Shoot a few short clips in the environment that you intend to make the video. Take shots from a few different angles. Then, examine the video footage. Make sure that there is enough light to see the important action. Also, listen to the audio, and make sure that the "actors" will be able to be heard and that there is not a lot of background noise. In some situations, such as a school cafeteria, it may be necessary to amplify the voices of the key actors so that they can be heard over the background noise.

Limit distractions

When shooting the video, try to limit the amount of distractions included in the shot. Think about controlling the level of extraneous sounds in the environment, especially if the targeted behavior is a verbal one. Unless the video is meant to help someone desensitize to active environments, limit the amount of extra action in the video, so that the main action is the one the learner needs to attend to. Be mindful to shoot the exact behaviors that you want to see, so that you don't inadvertently chain in behaviors that were not intended as the behavioral goal.

Using multiple models and settings

When teaching a skill that you would like the individual to generalize, it will be helpful to shoot the video showing a variety of different variables. This could include the possibility of using different models (for video modeling), different individuals with whom interactions are taking place, different materials, different environments, etc.

Highlighting

Occasionally, it might be useful to do a close-up shot to highlight certain aspects of the video. For teaching emotions, for example, you may want to start with a wider shot (to set the scene), and then zoom in for a close-up on the individual's face to draw attention to the facial features. Be cautious in over-using the "zoom" function, as some individuals have become disoriented and unable to continue watching videos with too much camera movement or scene shifting, due to sensory processing differences.

Another way to highlight relevant information is by pausing or freezing a video frame at a particular spot that you want the individual to pay close attention to while viewing the video. Using the example of teaching emotions, the video could be paused at a specific moment and the important facial characteristics could be highlighted for the individual. Some individuals put stickers on television monitors as a means of demonstrating knowledge of the relevant information. Note: before doing this, make sure that putting stickers on the monitor will not cause damage to the screen.

Background music, changes in sound, and voice-over

Another way to highlight relevant information is to add text, music, and voice-over dubbing. This is something that falls under the category of "knowing your learner." Watch the individual watching videos. Figure out if the person pays more attention when these types of effects are used. There may even be times you will want to turn off the sound all together when the individual needs to pay close attention to the physical actions within the scene.

CHAPTER THREE

Enhancing life and promoting competence

Address and heal

Central themes that have arisen among autistic self-advocates include feelings of being misunderstood by society; feeling like outsiders; and experiencing misjudgment and maltreatment at the hands of teachers, families and strangers (Gassner 2009, Williams 2009, Rubin 2004). Video technology can be used to address, heal and prevent such occurrences in the lives of those with autism.

Celebrate, document, and connect

Video technology can be used to celebrate a person, to document their life and to connect with friends and family, as well as a means of introduction to potential friends, new staff and co-workers.

EXAMPLES: Personal history

> "A positive approach invites people to enter into the same sort of relationship that most of us have and treasure: ongoing, with mutual affection and regard. In such relationships, we all make mistakes, are all in some ways inadequate, and yet it is not the level of success that makes the relationship so satisfying to the people involved; it is the ongoing commitment." (Lovett 1996)

Goal: To create a visual history (video, PowerPoint, or computer slideshow) of a person's life from their perspective. For many people with autism, especially those who do not access consistent communication, their history can get lost due to family and staffing changes and increased independence in how they live. Therefore, it can be vital for them to have a history of their lives to share with others and to view themselves, including the important people, places, and passions of their lives.

Implementation: Meet with the person to find out what is important to record. Most individuals will want a recording of people in their lives; some people might want a video of all the houses they've lived in or schools they've attended. For one young man, all the telephone poles that he could see from his various bedroom windows were important to him, and he requested these be videotaped.

Take a video of as much of the history of this person's life as is possible to access. This is an ongoing video, with additions being made regularly.

Considerations: Who will do the videotaping or picture taking? The individual may be interested in doing it themselves or may prefer someone else. How often will the individual view the video? Some people may prefer to view their videotape at crucial points in their lives, such as changes in living arrangements, schools, family or staff changes. Others prefer to view it at certain holidays (e.g., birthdays). How frequently will the video history be updated? There may be some natural times that the video is updated, such as school opening, the first of the year, or birthdays. Determine whether or not the person wants voiced words, music, written words, etc. added to the video. Captions or narration are helpful for individuals who do not consistently access communication, so that others can understand their video history.

EXAMPLES: **Happiness is ...**

> "The happier someone is, the less challenges they experience in life."
> (Gary LaVigna)

Goal: To create a visual compilation (video, PowerPoint or computer slideshow) of the elements in a person's life that bring them happiness and joy.

Implementation: Learn about the person's passions and interest areas. Plan with the person where and how to videotape or photograph these passions and interests. Leave the project open-ended for additions.

Considerations: It may be helpful to interview others who know the person well, in order to get additional clues. Consider the preferred modality for the individual (computer, video, DVD, handheld electronic device, etc.). Make certain that a person wants a visual compilation of their passions as some people have reported getting stuck on certain interest areas in a way that isn't useful.

Avoid using the compilation as a reward. Rather, consider having it available non-contingently for the sole purpose of enhancing the person's life. When referring to a preferred item one student said, "If you knew I loved it, you would have made me earn it" (Kluth 2003). It is optimal to avoid making the viewing of the video contingent on behavior, work production, etc.

EXAMPLES: Calming images

> "I loved repetition. Every time I turned on a light I knew what would happen. When I flipped the switch, the light went on. It gave me a wonderful feeling of security because it was exactly the same each time." (Barron 1992)

Goal: To create a visual record (video, PowerPoint, or computer slideshow) that can be viewed at those times when a person is anxious/agitated, or simply to make life better for the individual. Note: In a study that compares the heart rate of individuals with autism to individuals without autism, it was found that individuals with autism have a resting heart rate that is 20 beats per minute (average) higher both during baseline and when exposed to stressors (Goodwin et al. 2006).

Implementation: Learn from the person as well as from friends and family what is calming to the individual. Maybe, do some trial and error to determine what is most calming to the person. Videotape or in some other way visually compile calming images, sounds, and experiences. Make the visual compilation available to the person on an as wanted or as needed basis.

Considerations: Consider having preferred people say calming things to narrate the visual compilation. Consider unique passions that might be calming. For example, one individual found it calming to have a visual display of the Weather Channel available to him; another found it calming to have a photo display of deciduous trees on his handheld electronic device. Because access needs to be consistent across a variety of situations and environments, portability of the final product needs to be considered.

EXAMPLES: Celebrations and important moments

> "I spent almost 46 years of my life hating myself because I thought I was just too different for anybody else to love me. But I finally met somebody who loved me the way I was. In fact, she didn't want me to try to be anybody else but [me]." (Newport 2007)

Goal: To record events in a person's life that are celebratory and important from the individual's perspective.

Implementation: Possibly, do some pre-teaching of the concepts of individual values/importance and celebrations. Learn what is important and celebratory for the person and from others close to them. Determine how situations will be documented/recorded and what the process will be. Compile important and celebratory events. Provide access to the documentation/recording on an as wanted/as needed basis.

Considerations: Consider unique interests and passions when recording/documenting, and include those if the person wants them included. For example, important events in one person's life were Tom Brokaw's final newscast as an anchorperson and the first episode of *The Price is Right* after Drew Carey replaced Bob Barker as host. For another person, it was a celebration when he had (finally!) lined up every single one of the Pez dispensers in his collection.

EXAMPLES: Affirmations for building self-esteem

> "Sticks and stones may break my bones but words will wound forever." (Bloch 2003)

Goal: To create a visual compilation of affirmations for the purpose of building self-esteem and neutralizing negative messages the person might have received in their life.

Implementation: With sensitivity and respect, consult with the individual and compile the negative messages the person has heard. Determine how the visual compilation of affirmations will be done. Visually compile positive statements, images, and voices of others, which are in direct opposition to those the person has internalized. Make the recording/display available to the person on an as needed/as wanted basis.

Affirmations are stated positively (e.g., "I am calm" versus "I am not anxious"). Keep affirmations short, simple and clear. One positive manifestation of using affirmations is that the person may memorize them. This is more likely if the statements are concise.

Considerations: It is important that the affirmations used are truthful. For instance, if the person has heard "You're fat and ugly" and the person is overweight, it would not be a truthful affirmation to use "I'm skinny." It would, however, be a truthful affirmation to use "I am beautiful just the way I am."

Sometimes we can get a clue as to what negative messages a person has heard and internalized by what they say in a moment of stress. For instance, one person echoed negative comments made to him each time he perceived he'd made a mistake. For his affirmation compilation, his team found a positive for each of these negative statements and put it on a visual display for him to view regularly throughout his day.

The goal of this use of video technology is to counteract negativity and low self-esteem in a person's life. Therefore, consider making the positive statements/images particularly salient or visually pleasing to the person, so they will "stick out" in the person's mind. For instance, blue is the favorite color of one person for whom an affirmation PowerPoint was made, so she chose for the slides a blue background with ocean waves.

A variation to consider is to have a variety of people in the person's life say positive things about them, and to record these testimonials. If there is a particular personality or individual the person admires, consider having that person be interviewed for the recording.

EXAMPLES: Interviews

> "Autism is not something I have. It is integral to who I am. Eliminate the autism, and you eliminate me. When you say you want a cure, you are saying I should be put to death. Think about it." (Parrish S. Knight)

Goal: Record interviews of others with questions that are important to the person.

Implementation: Find out what is important to the person to know about others. Consider pre-teaching the concept of conducting interviews. Together with the individual, make a list of people to be interviewed (consider family, friends, staff, community members, admired others). Teach how to operate the video technology equipment that will be used to conduct the interviews, if the person is doing his/her own recording. Make the recording available on an as wanted/as needed basis.

Considerations: It may be helpful for the individual to have a script of questions, with cues for how to follow up the answers, such as "say thank you and smile," as well as any other personalized cues that might be helpful. For example, it was useful for one person to have a cue to take a deep breath after asking a question; for another person, it was helpful to have a visual reminder regarding how often to check the tape.

One way to determine what is important to a person is to pay attention to the kinds of things they ask or seek out. For instance, one person regularly asked about the color of people's cars after greeting them. Therefore, questions about whether or not a person owned a car and the car's color were important to include for this individual. For another, people's street addresses were important (not the street, just the numbers), so that was a question he asked others in his interviews.

This strategy can be used whether or not a person is verbal. If someone types to talk, for instance, they could type out the interview questions ahead of time and point to them one at a time. If a person uses pictures to communicate, those could be loaded onto a laptop computer or handheld electronic device with the interview words being typed in by another. The interview could be conducted by the person pushing the advance button to the next picture and question.

EXAMPLES: Connecting with others on the spectrum

> "Together, we share our stories and expertise, offering a glimpse into what we call the culture of autism. We do so in the hope that our greater community of families, professionals, and educators might discover new ways to integrate the information and perspectives we offer into their daily life and work, with the common purpose of building bridges of understanding across all segments of our autism community." (Hane and Paradiz 2009)

Goals: To provide a medium for people on the spectrum to connect with each other.

Implementation: Use online social networking and autism blogs to provide individuals a means with which to connect with each other. A number of people with autism have spoken about the benefits of using social networking websites such as Facebook and Twitter as a means of connecting with other people. These are by definition social in nature, but they are social in a way that is confined to the computer screen or a cell phone. It allows individuals with autism additional processing time. It conveys information in a visual way. A person can choose when to engage and when to pull back from engagement, unlike social interaction that occurs in-person or in "real time."

Considerations: Although social networking can be a wonderful way for individuals with autism to connect with others, it is important to educate them on the dangers of using social networking. Some people need to be taught the dangers of giving out personal information to people who are unfamiliar, meeting in person with someone who is unfamiliar, providing personal information about others in their life. An Internet safety course may be useful for someone new to social networking.

CHAPTER FOUR

Neurological supports

Help to access

One way to assist individuals with autism to access their skills on a more consistent basis is to videotape them when they are doing well and when their movement issues are less pronounced. Some individuals report having days/times where the movement and neurological difficulties their autism poses are decreased and other days/times where the difficulties of their autism are increased (McGinnity and Negri 2005). It can be helpful to record individuals when they are doing well, to show to them when they are having more difficulty accessing their skills.

One young woman had intermittent difficulty crossing thresholds of doorways, particularly when the doorways were going to and from the out of doors. Her family videotaped her on a day when her movement difficulties were not pronounced and she was moving fluidly through the doorways. On the days she got stuck, it was helpful for her to view herself on a more fluid day; sometimes, this assisted her in accessing more consistent motor movement through the doorways. The young woman reported that even when viewing the video didn't free up her movement, it nevertheless "gave her hope" to see herself in a more fluid time.

Movement is more fluid

As discussed in Chapter One, movement differences and diversity are often reported by and observed in autistic individuals. It causes us to pause and question if autism isn't primarily a syndrome of decreased and inconsistent access to skills and abilities due to intermittent neurological glitches. Supporting persons who have difficulty with transitions and consistent access to movement skills are two areas in which video technology can be useful.

For some, seeing themselves in fluid movement may assist them in being able to access this fluidity at those times they are experiencing challenges. For instance, a young man had difficulty getting in and out of the van that transported him to appointments. On a day he termed a "good movement day," he was videotaped getting on and off of the van, both when entering his appointment and when leaving it. The next time that he was "stuck" getting out of the van at an appointment, he was shown the clip of himself on the "good movement day" on the Flip video. While it didn't always work to free up his movement and it didn't free him up right away every time, it did allow him to get on and off the van with more consistency over time.

Increasing verbal skills

> "There are, on occasion, still times I want to talk, but I can't. I can try and try and try, but I can't talk. There is a fear holding me back. I do not know what it is I am afraid of, I only know that it is a feeling of fear unlike any other feeling of fear I have ever known. It is not that I do not want to talk, it is that I am unable to at that moment." (McKean 1994)

For people who speak, the problem with inconsistent access to skills can affect their verbal abilities. They may have times that they are able to talk/access their words and other times when they are not. It can be helpful to record individuals on a day when things are going well and their words are coming more easily for them, and show the video or PowerPoint to them on a day that access isn't as easy for them. This can be particularly helpful around a specific social situation, task or activity. If an individual is plagued with inconsistency in accessing their words in the social context of the lunchroom, for instance, it may be helpful to videotape them on a day when they are easily finding their words. Then have them review the video on a day which might be "glitchier" for them.

Showing alternative routes

Having more than one way to get places can be a compensation or solution for bodies that get stuck en route to class, school or community environments. It is one way to outsmart the neurology of autism that one high school student taught his staff. When he got stuck in one particular hallway on his way to class, he would take an alternate route. However, he only knew one alternate route and he sometimes would get stuck there, as well. His resourceful staff took their cue from him and designed multiple alternate routes to each class, in the event he got stuck in one of the routes. In order to show him the routes, they made a combination of a PowerPoint and video support, which they loaded onto his iPod Touch (i.e., by converting the PowerPoint to an MP4 file). They made a PowerPoint slide of the class he was going to and then videotaped each alternative route after the PowerPoint slide of where he was going. He could click on the slide of the next class and get alternate routes whenever he needed them.

EXAMPLES: **In-class transitions**

> "When my mom moved the furniture in the house I got very, very upset. I hated the change. I felt like I was not at home any more." (Paul McDonnell in Cohen 1998)

Goal: To assist the individual in making transitions within a classroom; from desk to floor or table to lab, for instance. This goal also includes making a transition from being supported by one staff to being supported by another.

Implementation: Take a short video of where the individual needs to go next and/or the activity central to the upcoming transition. For individuals who might be "stuck," it can also be useful to have a video clip of them successfully performing the next activity, so they can watch the video if they get stuck, to assist them in being able to execute the transition.

An individual with autism demonstrated his multiplication facts and was able to recite them when shown the flashcards by his teacher. He was able to recite all the correct answers for each multiple through 9x9. His teacher was very excited, as he had not been able to demonstrate this knowledge in the past. The next day, his teacher wanted to show off this newly demonstrated skill to others on his team. She used the same flash cards and the same cues, but he did not seem to know even one of the multiplication facts. When she asked him what was wrong, he replied, "Your hair is wrong." What had happened for him is that her hairdo had been learned into his demonstration of his multiplication facts. She had her hair down onto her shoulders when he demonstrated the knowledge. On the next day, she had her hair in a ponytail and he couldn't access his knowledge until she took her hair out of the ponytail. Once she did that, he was able to recite all his multiplication facts again. However, she wanted to be able to wear her hair in different styles. A video could help out this situation by showing him reciting his facts with her hair down and having him watch that on days she had her hair in a ponytail, or pulled back in a barrette. He might be able to generalize this skill and "transition" his knowledge from one setting (i.e., hairdo) to another.

Considerations: The filming of this video should resemble the typical transition as closely as possible. Consider, for example: which staff members will be present; the desk/chair where the individual will be sitting; peers who will be nearby; what (if any) communication opportunities will be present; how the individual is expected to participate in activities.

EXAMPLES: **Transition from elementary to middle school**

> "Nothing seemed constant. Everything appeared to be always changing."
> (Jerry Bemporad in Cohen 2006)

Goal: To assist the individual in making the transition from elementary to middle school with as much ease as possible, being able to carry over and access the full breadth of their current skills (movement fluidity, social and communicative, as well as academic). A video of this type can also be used with changes going from room to room, building to building, house to house, or job to job.

Implementation: Videotape the subsequent environment (i.e., middle school) for the person to watch beforehand.

For one student who was transitioning from elementary to middle school, it was useful to videotape the entire sequence of arriving at school, going to his locker, and then walking the hallway to each class in the identical manner to when he would begin middle school. He watched the video over the summer to help him visually prepare for his transition to sixth grade. A week or so before school started, his parents took him to the school and together they walked his schedule from classroom to classroom. According to his parents, the student's transition into sixth grade went smoother than the grade to grade transitions in elementary school, a process which had not included the use of video foreshadowing.

Considerations: Think about environmental structure; class switches; new routines (bus, locker, lunch). The same things changing or different things being named the same (e.g., lunch looks very different in middle school than it does in elementary school). Consider the increase in class size or number of teachers. Schedule differences (e.g., no recess; starting/ending times of day).

Other ways to address the same goal: conduct an internet research on middle schools; walk the path of what they are going to see in subsequent environment; edit together current environment and subsequent environment; if the school has a website, have the individual view the middle school online.

EXAMPLES: Access to skills

> "The symptoms and the continuum of autism are consistent with difficulties in the dynamics of movement." (Donnellan and Leary 1994)

Goal: To increase consistent access to abilities and skills.

Implementation: Videotape or otherwise record the person on a day when they have optimal access to their abilities and skills. This might be determined with the person, reporting that their thoughts are moving fluidly.

If the person is unable to provide this information, the days/times when there is more fluidity can be determined by observing the person for some of the following occurrences: increased speech, or less dysfluency in their speech; increased access to their augmentative communication device/system; increased ability to access a variety of environments; increased ability to demonstrate skills/tasks; less overall "stickiness" (getting stuck in thought, words or motor patterns); less difficulty with transition between tasks and people, etc.

On a day/time the person is having difficulty making a particular transition, accessing their verbal skills, or accessing the full range of their abilities/flexibility, they're shown the clip of the day/time they were doing well.

Considerations: Using video technology in this way can open up avenues for people who may have access issues. One might employ this use of video technology for the following: academic tasks; verbal skills; nonverbal communication such as augmentative communication systems and facilitated communication; stuck motor movement; emotional regulation; sensory regulation; and all varieties of transitions.

It is important that the video clip of the person doing well is shown in a supportive manner. For instance, one might present the video and say, "I see your movement is giving you a hard time today; let's see if watching yourself when you were having a better day will help you free up." Compassion for the person who is experiencing the access difficulty is going to yield the most success in terms of relationship and, in turn, movement accessibility.

EXAMPLES: Supporting flexibility

> "Those of us who live in the autism circle would consider the notion of flexibility coupled with autism, as polar opposites." (Author unknown)

Goals: Using Internet search engines like Google to increase an individual's flexibility in cognition.

Implementation: To use this technique, you will have the person conduct searches on Internet search engines to expand their experience around specific concepts. It will be especially useful if you search for "images" within the sites.

We have used this in the past to help individuals with autism to expand their flexibility around how certain things look. This technique worked very well with one third-grade girl. We used the search engine method to help her to realize that there were a wide variety of things in the world that people called "lights" because her definition of what was a "light" was very narrow (only lights that shine white light). By simply searching for the word "light," she was able to see literally thousands of different images of "lights." After doing this technique once a day for about a week, her definition became much broader. She now understands that lights can in fact come in many different sizes, shapes, and yes, even colors.

Considerations: When using search engines of this type, it will be important to remember to have "safe" options on for younger individuals. Searches for seemingly harmless topics can sometimes bring up some age-inappropriate images.

CHAPTER FIVE

Skills to teach

What to teach

Video technology can be used to teach skills in all arenas of an individual's life. Whether an individual needs support in learning how to brush their teeth, do a math worksheet, learn a communication strategy for a particular situation, or understand the salient cues in street crossing, video technology can enhance the instruction.

Finding effective teaching strategies for individuals with autism has been a common discourse in research over the years (Siegel, Goldstein and Minshew 1996). Part of the dilemma lies in determining what to teach. One element that impacts this decision is that many individuals with autism have difficulty generalizing skills taught from one situation to another. Teaching in the natural environments where the skills will be used is a remedy that has been discussed and implemented by many well-respected teachers. Because each individual possesses a unique learning style, it is important to consider how the person learns when determining what to teach.

Collaboration

What does the individual want to learn? If an individual is engaged in determining the goals for their education, there is a better chance the goals will be reached. Collaborating with individuals on their Individual Educational Plans (IEPs), Individual Support Plans (ISPs) or similar goal-setting documents also breeds respect into the process.

Usefulness

It is important to ask ourselves what the usefulness is of any skill/activity we are teaching. As individuals grow older, we need to consider subsequent environments in which they or their families hope they will be accessing, and teach to that future. It may be necessary to let go of some so-called "developmental goals" in lieu of goals that are more functional in nature and which will lead to increased independence for the individual. This is especially true regarding activities of daily living (ADLs). Skills such as grooming, dressing and taking care of one's clothing; functioning in the community; cooking for oneself, etc., may be important goals for even the most academically gifted individuals with ASD. Sometimes families are equipped and able to take on teaching such skills. Other times, however, families need assistance from the school in teaching these skills. Goals that address ADLs need to become part of the IEP/ISP.

When teaching any skill, it is important to have a notion of where the individual is currently functioning. This is more easily determined with academic goals. However, it is imperative that a teacher know exactly how an individual functions on ADLs, as well. One way to obtain this knowledge is to break the task down via a task analysis and see how the individual performs the skill without prompting (Falvey 1989). This will give teachers a starting point for the individual. It has been well documented that individuals with autism acquire and access skills at a more rapid and consistent rate when taught systematically. It is crucial to build consistent cues and correction procedures into the process of addressing all the goals on the IEP, as well as setting up a reliable data collection system to document the individual's progress.

There are sets of skills to be taught across life situations, such as social skills, communication, and sensory and emotional regulation. A systematic means of teaching needs to be in place for the benefit of the individual. Video technology can be a component in that consistency.

Communication

EXAMPLES: Increasing speech

> "I learned to talk at 4. I didn't learn to communicate until 11 or 12." (Bill Donovan in Cohen 2006)

Goal: To assist the individual in acquisition of language and fluency.

Implementation: If the individual is echolalic, videotape them using single word responses. For example: "I" / "want" / "ball." Using Movie Maker or other editing software, sequence the individual responses into a string making a complete sentence. Show the completed sequence of words to the individual in context. For individuals with more language, videotape peers using language for requesting, commenting, asking questions, etc. Show the video to the individual prior to the functional and appropriate time to use the language.

Considerations: Research has supported that all of the variables in stringing together language do not have to be consistent for success. For example, if you are videotaping singular responses on different days, clothing and staffing may be different (Buggey 2008). Consider the length of the utterance of the targeted response. If an individual is currently requesting using one-word utterances, videotape sequences of 2-3 words. If the individual consistently is using two- and three-word phrases, videotape additional word phrases. Once the individual is using an utterance length longer than the initial baseline, videotape the individual using the phrases. If the individual regresses at all, show the videotapes of them using the larger word phrases.

EXAMPLES: Volume of voice

> "I am like Data, the android man, on 'Star Trek, the Next Generation.' As he accumulates more information, he has a greater understanding of social relationships. I am a scientist who has to learn the strange ways of an alien culture." (Grandin 1995)

Goal: To assist individuals in regulating the volume of their voice to match what is appropriate for the setting.

Implementation: Identify several situations in which you want to demonstrate appropriate volume of voice. You may want to begin with situations that have a stark contrast (i.e, classroom vs. cafeteria). Videotape scenario with peers and/or individual. Compare similarities and differences to each situation. Identify important cues to situations that determine appropriate volume of voice.

Considerations: Consider supporting the video with additional visual cues (like a voice volume thermometer).

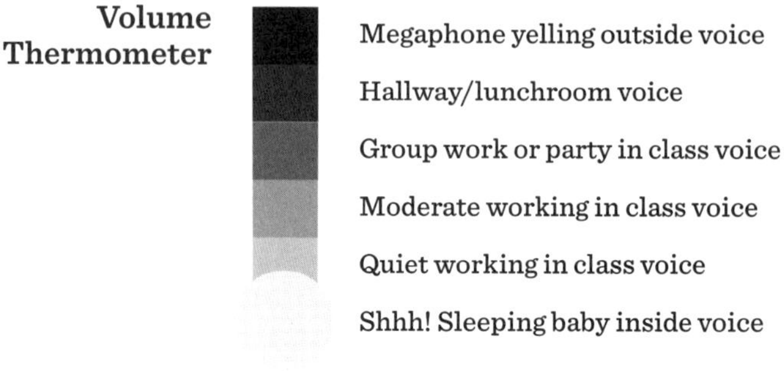

EXAMPLES: Conversation

> "I would often talk on and on about something that interested me ... I really was not interested in discussing anything; nor did I expect answers or opinions from the other person, and I would often ignore them or talk over them if they interrupted." (Williams 1992)

> "Three autistic boys aged 6-7, observed videotaped conversations consisting of 2 people discussing toys. Subsequent assessment of the boys using untrained topics of conversation, new stimuli, new persons, and other settings indicated that the children learned through video modeling, generalized their conversational skills, and maintained conversational speech over a 15-month period." (Charlop and Milstein 1989)

Goal: To increase conversational skills.

Implementation: Identify peer/peers with whom the individual is comfortable when initially teaching the art of conversation. Identify topic of interest to both conversation partners. If needed, use visual supports (index cards) to provide scripts, questions, and/or comments, which can be used to engage in conversation.

Support the give and take of conversation with visuals, such as: a "talking stick" which the speaker holds when it is her turn to talk; a card that is green that says "talking" and a card that is red that says "listening" and even one that is yellow that says "thinking"; "go" sign for the speaker and "stop" sign for the communication partner. Establish how many turns will take place in the conversational exchange.

Videotape the conversation and/or videotape others in conversation. When watching the video, pause during each process and highlight important skills

Considerations: Capitalize on areas of high interest to engage the learner in conversation. Kluth and Schwarz (2008) suggests that "fascinations, areas of expertise and strengths can be used to develop a relationship with the student and expand social opportunities."

EXAMPLES: Using an augmentative communication device

> "You might think that these individuals are mentally retarded or have no verbal skills, but in fact, they're not mentally retarded. They really understand what is going on and if they utilize a communication device, they can really communicate what they are thinking and feeling." (Hollander 2007)

Goal: To increase conversational skills through the use of an augmentative communication device.

Implementation: Using an augmentative communication device can be a very complex task. Determine which aspect you wish to teach (e.g., beginning to use the device, turning it on, etc., vs. more complex steps with multiple layers). Storyboard the steps involved. Videotape the sequence in the natural setting. Film from the perspective of the user. Show them the video before a conversational exchange within the natural environment.

Jack was a high school student who did not have a functional way to communicate his wants and needs to others. An evaluation was done for an augmentative device. When one was selected the staff videotaped the first steps in using the device and showed the videotape 6-8 times per day. They also showed him the videos prior to using the device. Jack's attention to the videos was high and his fluency with using the device was accelerated.

Considerations: When first using the device it is optimal to honor all of the requests that the individual initiates. After showing the video, follow the session with an activity in which the individual could use the device and access a preferred item. Videotape several different situations across settings, as the device will be optimally used across environments.

EXAMPLES: Watching scripts ahead of time

> "For me, thinking is seeing. In conversation, a word or group of words will bring up a set of pictures that logically lead to another set of pictures, like

> a 'domino effect.' If too many words lead to too many pictures, then my mind can, and usually will, shut down." (Heidi Kunisch in Ariel and Naseef 2006)

Goal: To increase expressive communication abilities by watching scripts ahead of time.

Implementation: Within the structure of a PowerPoint presentation, social situations can be illustrated and supplemented with conversation bubbles that provide the individual with possible topics of conversation, possible responses to greetings/closings, and when and how to take turns within the conversation. Starting this process with a PowerPoint gives the individual more control over the timing than with a video. It can slow down the rate of a typical conversation. Doing this allows for processing delays and lets the individual move at a pace with which they are comfortable.

When filming the video, start with a focus on "what" to say. You may want to include several possibilities of phrases. For a greeting, for example, you may want to show several ways to greet someone: "Hi," "How ya doing," "Hey." This will increase the individual's speed of generalization and help them be more natural in their greetings. After the individual has the "what" to say down, you can practice other things such as timing and delivery.

Considerations: As the learner becomes familiar with possible scenarios and responses, you may want to supplement the PowerPoint with a live video. This may assist the individual with timing and proximity and bring these skills closer to real life scenarios.

EXAMPLES: **Determining interest**

> "I remember my mother telling me not to do things I love. [My parents were always] interrupting me and interfering with me." (Barron and Barron 1992)

Goal: To increase communication skills in the area of receptive language abilities; determining interest.

Implementation: Many individuals with autism have topics of high interest about which they love to converse. Consider developing the ability to monitor/discriminate engagement in high interest topics by teaching the individual to determine when it is "ok" to engage in the high interest topics, and when it is not. Determining interest levels of topics with their peers is essential. The intricacies of identifying the subtle cues that peers deliver can be a daunting task. Using a PowerPoint presentation and/or video to highlight and identify facial cues and body language can be helpful.

Considerations: Assist the person in developing additional topics of conversation that may be of interest to peers. Resource: *The Model Me Conversation Cues* DVD (modelmekids.com) features middle and high school students demonstrating social skills at school and in the community. Each scene lasts between 30 seconds and 3 minutes, depending on the chapter. Storyboards summarize the rules taught. Two of the topics included in the video are "Cue: Interested" and "Cue: Not Interested."

EXAMPLES: Reading facial cues

> "I had tried to memorize people's expressions for the sole purpose of not saying the wrong thing at the wrong time. I could see happy (a smile), sad (tears), or angry (a lowered point brow). I thought all human interaction was based on these three." (Ariel and Naseef 2006)

Goal: To increase the ability to read facial cues from communication partner.

Implementation: There are many ways that one can communicate without ever saying a word. Simple gestures, facial expressions, body language and proximity can alter the intent behind every word spoken. In fact, entire back and forth conversations can occur without either communication partner ever saying a word. Nonverbal cues can subtly change the meaning of spoken words. A simple phrase, such as "Wow, look at that outfit she has on today" can have multiple meanings depending on the inflexion and body language of the speaker. The person speaking may really like your outfit. However, subtle or sometimes not-so-subtle nonverbal cues, such as a shift in facial expression, a change of voice tone, a roll of the eyes, can express the exact opposite meaning. Reading these facial cues can be intimidating.

Videotaping the subtleties of facial cues can be helpful. Videotape interactions, play the videotape, pause at moments you wish to review and highlight the different facial differences and their meaning.

Considerations: Analyze the setting (e.g., crowded mall vs. individual interactions) in which you are teaching. Areas that have a higher level of distraction sometimes make it more difficult for the person to access the information previously taught. This can affect their ability to read subtle cues in others. When teaching people to read facial cues, if using a video, pause and highlight the different cues by using a transparency to cover the face. Then, with an erasable marker, highlight and outline the specific cues (raising of the eyebrows, pulling down corners of the mouth, etc.).

Emotions

EXAMPLES: Identifying emotions in oneself

> "I just CAN'T understand human emotions, no matter how hard I try." (McDonnell 1993)

Goal: To recognize and identify emotions in oneself.

Implementation: Many individuals with autism can identify the "black and white" of emotional states within themselves yet have difficulty with the "shades of grey." There are many tools that can be used to teach the different emotional states, e.g., barometers, lotto games with match to sample, a mirror, etc. After selecting an appropriate tool, it is important to collaborate with the individual to identify the personalized language of each emotional state. To supplement the visual aid, videotape the scenarios which incorporate the intricacies of each state. The video can be supplemented with PowerPoint slides that have still pictures identifying each individualized emotional state of the person with autism. For example, when a person and/or peer is working at their table, allow them to look at a mirror while setting up a context for a particular emotion, such as telling a joke. If they smile or laugh you can say, "Look who's happy." You can also have the person attempt to imitate your expressions in the mirror. Videotape this format and compliment it with a PowerPoint presentation of matching facial expressions to their corresponding label.

Considerations: When videotaping, consider highlighting facial expressions, body positioning, body movement, tone of voice, choice of words and rate of speech. Use social stories (Gray 2010) that introduce emotions. To assist with generalization and identification of emotions expose the individual to the verbal label and picture in context.

EXAMPLES: Identifying emotions in others

> "I wanted to understand emotions. I had dictionary definitions for most of them and cartoon caricatures of others... I also had trouble reading what other people felt." (Williams 1994)

Goal: To recognize and identify emotions in others.

Implementation: Difficulty recognizing and identifying emotions is often paramount for people with autism. They can miss the facial cues that neurotypical individuals rely on to gauge the moods of others. There are many ways to teach identification of emotions in those around us: games (e.g., bingo, charades), emotions scrapbooks, people watching, etc. Another method is to have the person watch video clips. For example, in Disney's *The Lion King* there are many moments that highlight extreme emotions of happiness, sadness and anger. Stop each clip when an emotion is demonstrated. Point out to the individual the important facial cues of the corresponding emotion, such as raised eyebrows in a surprised expression. Videos can be replayed for multiple trials.

Considerations: Consider developing a social story (Gray 2010) that introduces emotions. Start with the emotion of "happy" first. Provide exposure to the verbal label and picture in context.

An excellent resource is *Mind Reading: The Interactive Guide to Emotions* (Jessica Kingsley Publishers 2007), a reference work covering the entire spectrum of human emotions. The software covers over 412 emotions, each one performed by six different people. Mini-stories provide context. (The voices have an English accent and use some vocabulary and cultural references specific to the UK. We have found this to be an important and invaluable resource for teaching emotions to children and adults with autism.)

EXAMPLES: Video scrapbook of emotions

> "The more I wanted to say or show something, the more my own Exposure Anxiety [see glossary] was tuned in, hanging on my every expression. My body, my facial expression, my voice and my words were pulled about by some wild horse inside of me. I'd want to say I was sad, my face would be beaming. I'd want to sit calm and still and enjoy a sense of company, my body would be propelled into wild diversion responses demonstrating discomfort and hyperactivity. I'd try to tell someone I liked them and swear

> at them, try to show caring and be compelled to do something to repel them." (Williams 2008)

Goal: To increase expression of emotions in oneself and understanding of emotional expression in others.

Implementation: An effective strategy that has been used to teach emotional expression in oneself and others is to create a personal emotions scrapbook (Attwood 2007). This is done by having an individual collect pictures of items that make the person happy, sad, mad and worried. The pictures can be supplemented with facial expressions of the corresponding emotion. Pictures can be found online, in magazines, and from personal photo albums and digital collections. Hint: to find photos of anger/sadness, sporting magazines are a good resource, as "the agony of defeat" is often depicted.

A video scrapbook of emotional expressions can also be created. This can be done by videotaping the person or peer playing with items that make them happy and then highlighting the facial expressions and body language that parallel the emotions. When the video is playing, pause the video and highlight the intricacies of the emotion by using a transparency placed over the TV or computer screen and using an erasable marker to draw over or exaggerate the expression. For some individuals, it may be useful to have still frames of the videotaped facial expressions which can be used to match and identify emotions when the video is paused, thus combining the emotions scrapbook idea with a video scrapbook to teach emotional expression.

Considerations: Determine if you are teaching emotions in the student or in others. It is best to not teach both simultaneously. The person might have a preference about what might be easier for them. Consider having the student interview others about what makes them happy, sad, mad, afraid, and videotape their responses.

Sensory regulation

EXAMPLES: Desensitization

> "We live in the midst of that hyperactivity to sound that so many observers have noted. Jessy has learned to control the intensity of her reac-

tions to the clicks and buzzes and hums with which the twentieth century surrounds us. But she still notices them." (Ariel and Naseef 2006)

Goals: To desensitize potentially distressing events for individuals with autism.

Implementation: Identify potential stressors for the person. Ask them what is stressful, providing a non-verbal way for response if the person does not speak.

A high school student was stressed by walking in the halls during passing times. His stress manifested itself as a "stuckness" in his body. His support team videotaped the students passing in the halls between classes and downloaded it onto his iPod Touch with a reinforcing video from YouTube at the end of the hall passing video. This helped the student's stuckness, as well as his sense of feeling overwhelmed when walking to his classes in the crowd of students. The positive YouTube clip at the end of each hall change served as a positive for him to see each time he arrived at a class and/or viewed the passing video.

Considerations: Once a stressful situation is identified and sequenced via video or PowerPoint, it can be useful to insert a highly reinforcing event or object at the end of the stressful situation to which the person is being desensitized. This makes watching the video of the stressful event more tolerable and positive. It can be helpful to incorporate a personal passion or interest into the clip. This will make the overall experience of watching the video more enjoyable and may also provide a neurological "trick" for the individual: when he thinks of the stressful event, the passion may be paired with it and reduce the stress automatically.

An elementary school student was fearful of squirrels, making it stressful for him to go outside. His staff made a video of the student walking outside, focusing on the squirrels and where their nests were located, etc., to provide some potential predictability about where the squirrels might run. It was pointed out that the squirrels tend to run away from humans. A passion was added to the narrative, which for this student was the letter "C." He loved that letter and often put it at the beginning of words that didn't start with "C" just because he liked to make and see that letter. So, the letter "C" (i.e., a pleasurable passion for this student) was incorporated into the squirrel video (i.e., frightening, worrisome) by having a constant "C" in the frame. The video was titled "C Meets Squirrel."

EXAMPLES: **Sensory support routines**

"After reading Temple Grandin's autobiography ... someone asked me if I thought a cattle chute would have helped me. I said I didn't need a cattle chute, I needed an orientation manual for extraterrestrials. Being autistic does not mean being inhuman. But it does mean being alien." (Jim Sinclair in Schopler and Mesibov 1992)

"A diet of sensory activities can do many things for a child over a period of time. It can calm an over-aroused or active child, increase the activity of an under aroused/passive child, prevent uncomfortable reactions to sensory input, reduce sensory seeking (self-stim) behavior, increase productivity and comfort for the child, and teach the child self-regulation strategies." (Davis and Dubie 2004)

Goals: To increase regulation strategies and supports.

Implementation: When looking at what routines (sensory strategies) to teach someone, it is important to first consult with an occupational or physical therapist who is specifically trained in sensory integration therapy and has assessed a sensory profile of the individual and given recommendations for sensory supports. After identifying the appropriate sensory supports, videotape the sequence of supports from beginning to end. Consider supplementing the video with visual supports of each activity and/or step. Prior to the individual starting a routine, show the video.

Considerations: Remember that sensory supports can change over time for individuals. Make a PowerPoint presentation using pictures of the sequence of steps involved with each identified component. Add text or audio cues for each step.

EXAMPLES: Square breathing

"Life is not about waiting for the storms to pass. It's about learning to dance in the rain." (Anonymous)

Goals: To support regulation by relieving stress and anxiety.

Implementation: Make a PowerPoint presentation using an animated picture of the "square breathing" technique. (Note: an example is included in the *Lights! Camera! Autism!* DVD supplement.) This is a strategy used to elongate and deepen the breath and bring about relaxation. The technique is as follows: Begin by slowly breathing in for five seconds as an arrow traverses one side of a

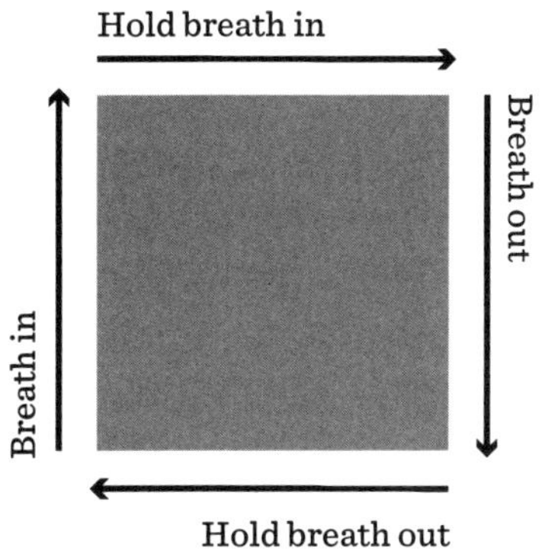

geometric square from bottom to top (it's helpful to count five Mississippi's). Hold the breath for five seconds as the arrow moves from left to right. Slowly breathe out for five seconds as the arrow goes from top to bottom. Hold breath for five seconds as the arrow moves from right to left. Repeat three times. Consider adding audio cues. This technique can be used individually or with groups.

Considerations: Videotape sequence and have individual watch before completing the square breathing exercises.

EXAMPLES: **Yoga poses**

> "[Yoga] gives the power to help [your child] develop a strong body, gain respect and love for herself, and discover a place of stillness and peace... It brings that marvelous inner light that all children have to the surface. Watch them shine!" (Wenig 2003)

Goals: To support overall emotional and physical regulation, via yoga.

Implementation: Videotape a series of predetermined yoga poses/routines. Before beginning the yoga routine, show the video to the individual. You may want to support the routine with visuals (e.g., a picture and written description for each pose/asana in the sequence) and/or PowerPoint presentation of the routine. There are also many commercially produced yoga video routines available that are helpful for some individuals.

A girl who was deaf and autistic was having trouble learning yoga in class, despite the teachers using a signed script and still visual pictures, as well as live modeling of each pose. She also had intermittent physical support and facilitation of each pose. However, once a video of each pose was presented to her, with the videotaping happening from the back (i.e., instead of mirror image) she was able to learn the poses with more ease and much more quickly.

Video technology can be helpful not only in learning yoga techniques, but also in accessing them and generalizing them across environments.

One young man with autism took a yoga class, which provided a video of each of the poses, in the order they were presented in class. The video was shot in class (a recognizable context). When this young man became agitated at home, one of the calming choices on his choice board was doing yoga. His staff assisted him in getting the video and putting it in, and then, he was able to independently do the yoga routine. He was not able to do the routine without the video, which suggests it is the video that supports his access to the yoga postures. Yoga visibly calmed his agitation and the video allowed him to access to the postures.

Considerations: Yoga can be taught and used as a relaxation technique and can be incorporated as calming activity before or after transition times. Some individuals experience movement differences, which make it difficult for them to access the motor skills necessary to complete yoga postures. Something that has been useful for people with accessing difficulties: Before starting a yoga class, have a videotape of the routine that they will be doing so they can practice and become familiar with the instructor, the music that accompanies the routine (if any), and the setting in which the yoga class will take place.

Hint: Another helpful technique for individuals who might be having difficulty accessing the motor components necessary for yoga postures is to begin by teaching them partner poses with a peer. Sometimes, the physical feedback of another's body, as well as the mirror image that many partner postures offer, can be a solution to the access issues.

EXAMPLES: **Developing new responses to stressors**

> "Many observers, including parents of individual with ASD have noted that no two individuals with autism are alike. They grow, develop and behave in unique ways, just as the population of youngsters and adults who are free of this disorder do. In particular, individuals with autism manifest anxiety and stress reactions." (Baron et al. 2006)

Goals: To support emotional and physical regulation.

Implementation: Identify individual stressor and/or stressful situation. Determine alternative, more life-enhancing response and what information is needed. Videotape stressor with alternative response. For example, if a student becomes anxious around hamsters, a staff could videotape the hamsters and videotape the student doing something that calms him, such as a relaxation routine or pushing the wall for proprioceptive input. The staff could then splice the two clips together. The next step in implementation would be to have the student

Push the wall

watch the videotape before the stressor occurs. In the example above, the student would watch the videotape before going into a room with a hamster in it.

A young adult student was having difficulty with a staff member. He was targeting her with nasty comments and reported having thoughts of wanting to hurt her. Further investigation and questioning revealed that she had made a face when he asked her something. He didn't understand the meaning of the facial expression, so he assumed it was disapproval and judgment. The young man was encouraged to ask the staff person what she was thinking when she made that face. He learned she was thinking something through that he had asked her: that was her facial expression indicating "deep thought." The young man was then encouraged to videotape himself interviewing her about her facial expressions, having her make various faces while simultaneously explaining what she meant by each expression. This information and process of using video technology allowed the young man to let go of his misperception. The relationship between him and this staff person greatly improved.

Considerations: Sometimes the stressor is a situation or an object. Sometimes it is a person. If the individual is in adolescence it can sometimes be a person they have a crush on or a peer with whom they have had a past negative experience. When using video to support alternative responses to a stressor of any kind, the student needs to have the alternative response in their repertoire before watching the videotape of the stressor so that watching the videotape does not create anxiety. It is also important that the student be part of the process in making the videotape and determining specifics about the stressor. When the process is collaborative it can empower the student; if it is not collaborative, it runs the risk of creating further stress for the student.

Social skills

EXAMPLES: Perspective taking

"Someone who has much better inherent communication ability than I do but who has not even taken a close look at my perspective to notice the

Universal "no" symbol

Thumbs down

enormity of the chasm between us tells me that my failure to understand is because I lack empathy." (Jim in Cesaroni and Garber 1991)

"World people have just as much trouble taking the perspective of autistic people as the reverse. However, we don't often hear that world people lack empathy or are unable to take another's perspective." (Judy Endow, personal conversation)

Goal: To increase awareness of the perspective of others.

Implementation: Identify the situation in which you wish to teach the individual to take into consideration the perspective of another person. Photograph each step. Sequence the pictures together in a PowerPoint presentation format to teach skill. Highlight the exchanges by supplementing the pictures with thought bubbles and individualized reactions/thoughts.

Considerations: It may be important to utilize visual cues in the form of thought bubbles, talking bubbles and waiting-your-turn bubbles, when teaching the skill. If you are going to represent an inaccurate interpretation, clearly and visually demonstrate that it is not the "right way." Perhaps using the universal "no" sign sustained throughout the entire portion of the inaccurate interpretation.

Videotape a session with the individual using *Comic Strip Conversations* (1994) by Carol Gray. Gray's system uses simple comic book drawings and balloon dialogue to map out the interpersonal give-and-take of a conversation for people who are challenged by social situations and the complexity of needing to rapidly summarize information and verbally share it.

EXAMPLES: **Inviting another to play**

"I am not asking for my child to be the life of the party, or a social butterfly.

I just want her to be happy and have some friends of her own. She is a wonderful kid, and I hope someday others can see that." (Anonymous)

Goal: To increase social interaction skills by teaching an individual to invite another person to play with them.

Implementation: Determine the setting in which play will naturally occur. Identify peers who are interested in play interaction. Videotape the exchange of the individual/peer inviting another peer to play. Consider supporting this interaction with the use of visuals (e.g., scripts, cue cards). Make sure the language is clear and specific for the interaction.

Considerations: Take into account the individual's sensory sensitivities when setting up the play situation: auditory (e.g., number of individuals, noise levels); visual (e.g., movement of individuals in the play area, clothing types); tactile (e.g., if outside, wood chips, playground equipment, sand; if inside, sand table, water table, manipulatives); smell (e.g., outside air if on playground). Make sure the environment is optimal for social interaction. Often areas that are too noisy, too crowded and/or too visually distracting hinder the process of engagement. When first teaching this skill, consider having the activity that will follow the invitation be one that is of high interest to the individual. Dyads and small groups tend to foster more success and intimacy than larger groups. Consider using a PowerPoint presentation to outline each step of the invitation as a supplement to the video, with thought bubbles added to the still visuals to enhance the process.

EXAMPLES: Greeting

"I was never *quite* sure how to handle certain situations. It is very difficult ... to know exactly when to say something, when to ask for help, or when to remain quiet ... Life is a game in which the rules are constantly changing without rhyme or reason." (Anne Carpenter in Schopler and Mesibov 1992)

Goal: To increase social participation and support development of meaningful relationships by teaching greeting skills.

Implementation: Storyboard the steps involved. Videotape the sequence of steps to initiate a greeting. Identify the place and time for instruction. Make sure the environment is free from distractions and allow for wait time.

Kayla, a third-grade student with autism, had a difficult time saying hello to her friends and teachers. She also struggled with conversational starters that expanded beyond "hi." Kayla's speech and language therapist at school utilized the application Stories 2 Learn on her iPod Touch by creating visual scripts, which gave Kayla a step-by-step sequence of the language she could use to engage with her friends and peers. She utilized the iPod Touch before approaching her peers and eventually did not need the visual aid to intiate and expand her conversational exchanges.

Considerations: One aspect to consider is the length of exchanges when videotaping. For some individuals a simple "hello, how are you" will be ample and for others a more complex 3-4 turn exchange may be optimal. Also, the type of interaction (with peer, adult, member in community) will need to be pre-determined. Interactions vary depending on the setting. Written scripts may be an effective visual support to enhance the interaction. Having the scripts on index cards allows the individual to reference them during an interaction.

EXAMPLES: **Closing**

> "I simply didn't know... what talking was for... Speech therapy was just a lot of meaningless drills in repeating meaningless sounds for incomprehensible reasons. I had no idea that this could be a way to exchange meaning with other minds." (Jim Sinclair in Schopler and Mesibov 1992)

Goal: To increase social participation by teaching individuals how to end a conversational exchange.

Implementation: Storyboard the steps involved (e.g., look down, drop voice level, step away from communication partner, pack up personal items, etc.). Videotape the sequence and/or brief communication exchange. Identify the place and time for instruction. Teaching this skill in an area free of external distractions may be preferred (i.e., quiet classroom space vs. crowded hallway).

Considerations: The context of the interaction (i.e., whether the exchange is with peer, adult, or co-worker) determines language and degree of formality. For example, when saying goodbye to a peer, one may use contemporary slang such as "catch ya later" or a simple head nod. This type of closing might be less appropriate, however, for a teacher or job supervisor. Supplement the video with a PowerPoint presentation to highlight skills such as how far to stand from your communication partner, where to place gaze, potential added gestures, etc.

EXAMPLES: Turn taking

> "Work to view my autism as a different ability rather than a disability. Look past what you may see as limitations and see the gifts autism has given me. I may not be good at eye contact or conversation, but have you noticed I don't lie, cheat at games, tattle on my classmates, or pass judgment on other people." (Notbohm 2005)

Goal: To increase social participation by teaching turn taking.

Implementation: Storyboard the steps involved. A PowerPoint presentation can be supplemented with pictures in a small photo album, which the individual can access in the moment. Begin teaching the skill using highly preferred activities. Teach the skill in a natural setting.

Considerations: Begin with a familiar activity. This is to avoid teaching both a new social skill (i.e., turn taking) and a new activity at the same time.

Mark and Katie are classmates of Frank, a third-grade student with autism. One afternoon Mark asked his teacher if he could play a game during indoor recess with Frank. Mark's teacher thought that would be a great idea as they had been working on Frank's turn taking skills and it would promote not only this skill but also his friendship skills. Frank's teacher first videotaped Mark and Katie playing a game that Frank was familiar with. She then showed the video to Frank, highlighting sections of turn taking between his peers. Next, a PowerPoint was created of the separate steps of turn taking during the game. Reinforcement was added for successful waiting between turns. Frank watched the video several days before playing the game with Mark. When Frank played the game, he kept the PowerPoint that his teacher had printed out next to him for reminders. Once Mark and Frank were successful in playing the game and taking turns, Katie joined in the game as well.

EXAMPLES: Joke telling

> "Through humor, you can soften some of the worst blows that life delivers. And once you find laughter, no matter how painful your situation might be, you can survive it." (Bill Cosby)

Goal: To increase social participation by teaching joke telling.

Implementation: Know your material and your audience. There are many "hidden curriculum" items related to joke telling, such as: make up of the audience; profanity vs. no profanity; and the age appropriateness of the joke. Even if you're ad-libbing, have a clear idea of where you're going. Not all jokes are appropriate for all gatherings. Do not ask for permission to tell a joke. Do not tell everyone how funny your joke is beforehand. Provide details the audience needs to know. Once you begin your joke, follow through to the punch line.

Considerations: Expose the individual to different styles of comedy and joke telling. You may want to show videos of stand-up comedians. Many individuals will need direct teaching and a rule structure around matching a joke to a particular audience. The importance of timing may need to be directly taught and repeatedly rehearsed. (Resource: "True Life: I Have Autism." A young man with autism and his journey to pursue his passion of comedy. MTV. 18 March 2007.)

Speech pathologist Jenny Potanos tells the following story: I was working with a fifth grade student with Asperger's syndrome. John had a difficult time with telling jokes, understanding them, understanding how to respond when others told them, etc. I worked with John on joke telling. As part of his "rewards" program he got to go down to the kindergarten and be a helper at the end of each day. One day I was in the kindergarten and he said to me, "Jenny, I want to tell the kids a joke." Of course I wanted to reinforce this since he was initiating the idea. When we got all of the kindergarteners sitting down John told an incredibly dirty joke (which we did not realize was a dirty joke until the punch line). The kindergarteners laughed uproariously even though they didn't understand the punch line. They had the pragmatics piece that you laugh when someone tells a joke. I didn't want to discourage John, but I wanted to use the teachable moment to let him know that kind of material was not okay for little kids. I pulled him aside and told him that it was a joke for "older people and not for little kids." That night I went home thinking all these kindergarten parents were going to call me and ask me why I let him tell that joke. But my phone only rang once and it was John's mom. She wanted to know why I told John to call his grandmother and tell her a dirty joke. Clearly all he had picked up on was "a joke for older people" piece. His grandmother was in her nineties and lived in a nursing home.

Adaptive living skills

EXAMPLES: Brushing teeth

> "I cannot emphasize enough the importance of a good teacher." (Grandin 1996)

Goal: To maximize independence by acquiring the self-care skill of brushing teeth.

Implementation: Storyboard the steps involved in the teeth-brushing routine. Videotape in the actual environment in which brushing will occur. Identify instructional cue (i.e., "Brush teeth") to begin the task.

Considerations: Environment, materials and sensory sensitivities can all play a role in the success of the video's use. Using an electric vs. manual brush for some individuals may cause disregulation due to the vibrating input and for some it may be a preferred means of input. It requires well-developed fine motor abilities to squeeze toothpaste from a container. Adaptations with type of bottle and/or tube may be needed. Some toothpaste products have strong scents or tastes. A product with no scent or a mild scent may be preferred. Often the type of toothbrush (soft vs. hard) needs consideration. Some individuals have oral sensitivities and cannot tolerate a hard brush.

EXAMPLES: Washing hands

> "I have been told many times that I am an exception, and that others will never be able to reach my potential. I find that ironic when I look at my past—a young boy who was not supposed to be able to learn anything. I guess I was classified as low functioning then. Now all of a sudden, I am high functioning. I am neither high functioning nor low functioning. I am who I am! I am Patrick Worth." (Patrick Worth)

Goal: To maximize independence by acquiring the self-care skill of washing hands.

Implementation: Storyboard the steps involved in the hand-washing routine. Videotape in the actual environment. Identify instructional cue (i.e., "Wash hands") to begin the task.

Jamie, a tenth-grade student with autism, was having difficulty initiating the individual steps of washing his hands. While he did not have difficulty with the motor planning of each step, Jamie would wait until verbally directed to complete each step. His teacher took pictures of each step and imported them into a PowerPoint presentation. Initially she stood next to Jamie and the computer's PowerPoint display when he was ready to wash his hands and prompt him through each step with the visual. The PowerPoint had sound built into the presentation. As Jamie became comfortable with the prompt from the computer, the sound was turned down each time until it was completely faded. Once the sound was faded, the pictures in the PowerPoint were the only stimulus. When Jamie was consistently responding to just pictures, the computer was faded out as well. Within a two-week period, Jamie was independently washing his hands. (Note: An example of this hand washing PowerPoint can be found on the DVD included with *Lights! Camera! Autism!*)

Considerations: If using a PowerPoint presentation to teach the skill, add text or audio cues.

EXAMPLES: Haircuts

> "I recall specifically one time when I walked into a Circus Cuts and was relieved to not have any people there. As the haircut progressed my son melted down and after thrashing, scratching and screaming I was blinded by hair, and the smock." (Garrett Butch 2010)

Goal: To assist the individual with autism in a basic self-care activity.

Implementation: As it may be difficult to use a self-model for this scenario, the best option is to use a peer model for videos of this type. Videotape a peer model receiving a haircut. Take time to show the haircut from different angles. Illustrate the fact that the peer is not being hurt and is remaining calm for the event. Then, show the video to the autistic individual before they receive their haircut.

A video model of haircutting was made for a seven-year-old with autism. The child would scream and cry when it was time to cut his hair. His parents tried everything they could think of to make the experience easier for the child. Eventually, they even tried cutting his hair while he was sleeping. A video model was filmed to assist the child in this process. In the model, a classmate and friend of the child is shown sitting and getting his hair cut. He is shown getting his hair cut with both a buzzer and a scissors. The friend is shown remaining calm while the haircut is happening. After the cut, the friend is shown standing up and brushing himself off. The video was shown to the child with autism before he received his next haircut. This video paired with some other desensitization (mom made one cut of his hair each day for a few weeks until it did not bother him any more) and now he can get his hair cut when needed. It is no longer an agonizing and torturous event for all involved. (See DVD Supplement)

Considerations: Remember to pick an appropriate model. You want to pick a model that is most like your target individual. You want to show the model receiving the same type of haircut that the individual will receive. Also, if possible, consider having your model be in the same setting and with the same hairdresser as your individual will be. Remember that there are many individuals on the spectrum who report that they have more feeling in their heads than many neurotypicals do. Some autistic people report that getting a haircut actually physically hurts them. If this is the case, allow the individual you are supporting as much control as possible over their haircutting routine.

EXAMPLES: **Doing laundry**

> "There's a lot more room in the world for good worker ants than queens." (Newport 2002)

Goal: To maximize independence by acquiring the self-care skill of doing laundry.

Implementation: Storyboard the steps involved. Videotape or photograph the washer/dryer sequence. Film in the natural environment or an environment where the equipment is as similar as possible to the washer and dryer the individual will be routinely operating. A visual to support the important components according to the type of clothing, water temperature and dryer setting may be beneficial. Some washers/dryers have printed or visual directions on the appliance. Identify the place and time for instruction; materials required for the task (e.g., laundry detergent, softener or dryer sheets, clothing sorted by lights, darks, colored and whites); and any additional supports such as a visual for sorting laundry; an adaptive device for folding laundry, etc.

Considerations: Environment, materials and sensory sensitivities can all play a role in the success of the video's use. Washers/dryers in the home today might be energy efficient front-loading models. If the individual is learning the skill in a top load machine that isn't consistent with the home environment, a mini-picture schedule of visual supplements (or separate videos) may be needed to support the difference in each environment. A PowerPoint presentation may be beneficial for each combination of clothing. For individuals who do not exhibit clear judgment skills, it will be important to have a measuring component in the task analysis, not only for the amount of detergent, but also for how full to fill the washer, how to determine when clothes are dry, and for sorting darks and lights.

EXAMPLES: **Setting the table**

> "I wanted to show that people like me can live a normal life and also that we're not what people think. Asperger's syndrome is not a life sentence. It's a blessing, not a curse." (A. Cowan)

Goal: To maximize independence by acquiring the self-care skill of setting the table.

Implementation: Complete a task analysis and storyboard the steps involved. Use visual supports to assist the individual in completing this routine. Visuals can be in the form of a flip picture book outlining the steps or a placemat at each setting that has outlined spaces for each item that needs to be placed on it.

Considerations: Determine whether or not the individual will gather all of the necessary table items before setting the table. Contributing factors may be location of table from cupboards, where dishes are held, individual's personal style, etc. For some individuals, it may be important to complete each place setting before moving on, while others may wish to set all of one item at a time (e.g., all the plates, then all the forks, and so on) moving around the table in repetition.

Fork Knife Spoon Spoon

The type of tableware needed for an occasion varies significantly depending on the situation. Visuals can be useful to clarify the type of tableware needed for the occasion. An example of a way to incorporate a visual is to develop a picture book outlining different types of occasions and what type of setting is needed for each. This would allow the individual a form of reference when identifying the correct tableware.

EXAMPLES: **Using the microwave**

> "That's the real problem with kids who struggle with learning. Some kids feel like they're stupid. I want them to know that they're not. They just learn differently. Once they understand that and have the tools to learn in their individual way, then they can feel good about themselves." (Charles Schwab)

Goal: To maximize independence by acquiring the self-care skill of using the microwave.

Implementation: Storyboard the steps involved. In teaching this task, it may be beneficial to consider using a PowerPoint of each step to show prior to beginning the task. Supplementing a PowerPoint with individual pictures in a small photo album, which the individual can access in the moment, may also be helpful. Begin teaching the skill using highly preferred foods, which the individual can eat upon completion of cooking. It is important to teach the skill in a natural setting.

Considerations: Individuals may need to be directly taught these related skills: Determining and using microwave-safe dishes; lid vs. covering dish with paper towel or plastic wrap; identifying items which need to be stirred halfway through; using hot pads to remove items after microwaving. Additionally, they may require visuals to support their use of the microwave (e.g., placing different colored dots numbered 1, 2, 3, etc., on each step on the microwave). There may be a need for instruction on how to prepare food prior to cooking (e.g., putting cocoa in the cup and stirring prior to placing it in the microwave). Some individuals may have sensory sensitivities to sound, requiring the use of sound blocking devices (e.g., earplugs or headphones) which would need to be included in the video. Location of the microwave may vary between home, school, and break room. If an individual is going to be using multiple microwaves, the skill may not necessarily transfer. Therefore, separate videos may be needed in each environment in which the individual will be using a microwave. Other individuals will be able to generalize the skill.

To teach the difference between express vs. manual settings on the microwave, it may be helpful to have a correlating visual support in the form of a book with the settings and times for each of the food items the individual typically heats up in the microwave. To teach different types of settings (defrost, reheat, 50% heat), additional visuals may be required to support an individual's understanding of when to re-heat versus defrost, etc. Locating and reading package directions (microwave directions vs. conventional oven directions) is another related skill to be included in the video, which will boost overall independence for the individual.

EXAMPLES: **Tying shoes**

> "How do I provide the right pull for him, neither too hard nor too soft? I first try to know who he is, what he himself needs, loves, hates, fears." (Irene Litherland in Ariel and Naseef 2006)

Goal: To maximize independence by acquiring the self-care skill of tying shoes.

Implementation: Do a task analysis and storyboard the steps involved. Videotaping from the perspective of the person tying the shoes, rather than an observer position, is often most successful for the learner.

In teaching younger children, the analogy of making bunny ears is often used. If the learner is a literal thinker, they may get stuck in this analogy, and be reciting bunny ears while tying shoes when much older, thus infantilizing them. Therefore, choose the strategy for teaching carefully, insuring it is longitudinally sound and will not work against the learner at a later date. It is important to know your learner.

Determine hand dominance, and begin videotaping on the side of the dominant hand (i.e., if right handed, videotape the right shoe being tied first; if left handed, begin with the left shoe being tied first).

Garrett, a second-grader with Asperger's syndrome, had for many years worn tennis shoes with Velcro straps because he could not tie his shoes. During the beginning of his second-grade year, Garrett expressed to his teacher an interest in learning to tie his shoes. He wanted to be just like "Joe," a friend who wore Nike tennis shoes with a "cool red swish." Garrett's teacher found a video on

YouTube which demonstrated this skill. He watched the video every day before practicing the skill. It took him three weeks to learn how to tie his shoes. Soon after he learned the new skill, Garrett's teacher surprised him with a new pair of Nike's with the "cool, red swish."

Considerations: It is important to consider the type of shoe (e.g., athletic vs. dress). Shoe laces are different according to the type of shoe and, therefore, the tying will feel differently. While it may be tempting to teach the skill of tying on a skill board first instead of on the actual clothing item, caution is suggested here. The presentation of the skill looks and feels very different on a board than on a shoe. Tying a shoe that is on the person's foot requires bending over and a different body position overall. For some individuals it may be important to teach the skill in context from the start.

School

EXAMPLES: Locker routine

> "I felt like the world was an ocean and I never knew which wave was going to knock me over next." (Newport 1999)

Goal: To maximize independence within the context of functional routines, such as a locker routine at school or in the community.

Implementation: Storyboard the steps involved. Once the routine has been established, videotape the entire locker routine. To minimize stimuli/distractions, have the individual enter the hallway where their locker is located prior to the other students. For some individuals it is important that the video be taken in the exact location that their locker is located. If the individual is transitioning into a new building and/or this is their first time using a locker, it may be helpful to practice the routine over the summer months as part of their transition plan.

One way that movement differences can manifest is that individuals can appear prompt dependent (Donnellan, Hill and Leary 2010). What happened for one student is that certain prompts appeared to be learned in as an integral part of executing his locker routine. Without the adult standing next to him saying, "Get your backpack; unzip your backpack; get your coat; put it on," etc., he stood still at his locker. At times, he would tell the adult what to say: "Say, 'get your backpack.' " Visual technology was very useful for this student. Together with his team, he put together a PowerPoint presentation of each step of his locker routine. Typed words and audio were added to each slide. The PowerPoint presentation was downloaded onto his electronic handheld device and he was taught to push the advance button after executing each step. A step was added that said, "Put your iPod Touch on the shelf in your locker." He didn't need to hold onto the device while he was juggling all his other personal items. This student no longer needs an adult standing next to him repeating each step of the locker sequence to him. On some days, he uses the handheld device for self-cuing and on other days, he doesn't seem to need it.

Considerations: Some aspects to consider before teaching a locker routine include: how to set up the locker (books on top, shoes on the floor or vice versa); color-coding books to match folders and notebooks for each subject; a visual of the daily schedule inside of the locker. The location of locker may be important for the individual's success. Sometimes the optimal locker location is at the end of a row or one with enough space so that the individual isn't bombarded by stimuli (e.g., bumped/jostled by students on either side) while trying to complete the locker routine.

EXAMPLES: **How to use a combination lock**

> "I think the fluidity of access to various places in the brain is dependent upon neurological movement between places. I'm no scientist, but have always been able to 'see' this inside of me. Sometimes my speaking is hindered; other times my thinking and sometimes my physical movement. The hardest is when thinking is not working smoothly. When that happens I have to line up one thought at a time, like train cars. I like it much better when my thoughts do not have to be methodically lined up, but are more fluid with colors coming in and out and swirling into unique and beautiful patterns. (My thoughts are in pictures and sometimes moving colors)." (Judy Endow, describing her experiences in relation to sensory and movement differences, January 25, 2009, personal communication on Facebook.)

Goal: To maximize independence within the context of functional routines, by using a combination lock.

Implementation: As students enter middle school, a new skill that is often needed is learning how to use a combination lock for their lockers. There will often be two separate locations in which they will need to use a combination lock (one locker for their books, school supplies and outer clothing, and another for physical education). Develop a task analysis of the individual steps needed in opening a combination lock. Videotape the process from the perspective of the individual opening the lock. Initially, you may want to develop a PowerPoint presentation of the individual steps and/or take still pictures accompanied with words to highlight the process.

Considerations: It will be helpful to assess the individual's preference and fine motor skills when determining whether to use a combination vs. key lock. One aspect to consider when using video technology in teaching how to use a combination lock is how much time is allotted to open the lock and gather materials. The location of the locker is an important consideration, especially for students who have sensory sensitivities. For instance, it may be helpful to have a locker on the end of a row or with an empty locker on either or both sides, to decrease the amount of jostling and sensory bombardment that the individual experiences while using their locker.

EXAMPLES: Circle time

> "My mind moves like lightning and my body like a cement truck. Yet, it is all I can do to stay sitting. My mind is like a freight train and I can't make it slow down and stop in time. I wish it was not so persistent in its moving." (Daniel McConnell in Young 2010)

Goals: To increase an individual's ability to engage in "circle time" with their peers.

Implementation: Video modeling is an effective means of teaching this skill. Shoot video of the class engaging in the behaviors that you would like your student to increase. Possible behaviors to catch on video might include: sitting with your hands in your lap; raising your hand when you have something to say; and listening to other people when it is their turn to talk. Most classrooms have some predictable routines that occur each day, such as calendar, weather, lunch count, roll call, daily oral language, current events, etc. It is helpful to include these in the video so that the individual can learn these predictable routines and be more competent in performing them when they occur in the classroom.

We used video modeling to help a second-grader engage more fully in circle time. He was having difficulty taking turns with the other children and always wanted to be the one that was called on first. We videotaped the child waiting while sitting in the circle (the shot was actually taken before the circle time began). Next we videotaped the teacher asking the class questions. Through editing, we made it appear that every time the teacher asked a question the child would sit and wait calmly for a few others to answer before he was called upon. After watching the video for a couple of weeks, we noticed a dramatic increase in the child's ability to sit and wait calmly while other children were called on in circle time. The wonderful thing about this situation was that this skill then generalized beyond circle time, to times when the children were at their desks as well.

Considerations: There may be multiple reasons why circle time can be difficult for autistic individuals, including sensory sensitivities. Consider giving the child with autism an assigned seat for circle time. Sometimes it helps if the student has a chair that they can sit in at circle, because it helps to define exactly what "their space" is. Sometimes a seat on the edge of the circle works best because it will limit the possibility of being accidentally bumped by other children at their sides.

EXAMPLES: Teaching academics

> "Teachers must be willing to not just give me a desk and then leave me to fill the chair. I need to be asked questions, and given time for my thoughtful answers. Teachers need to become a conductor, and guide me through the many places I may get lost." (Burke 2007)

Goal: To teach academics in a manner that is consistent, clear and motivating.

Implementation: Determine an academic task (probably from the IEP) that the individual is interested in learning (e.g., addition; reading sight words; math games; diagramming a sentence). Decide the methodology that will be used to teach the task. Videotape the instruction with either the individual, or a peer or video model.

Movement challenges may be misunderstood by others. This happened for one middle school student for whom math was a difficult subject. There were times when he could access his math abilities and other times when he couldn't. On the days he couldn't do math, his staff (mis)interpreted his behavior as "volitional." They made comments such as, "He is refusing to do his math today." It was helpful for this team to shift their perspective. Once the staff started thinking in terms of movement, they decided to videotape him on days he was able to access his math abilities. On days when he was having trouble coming to the table or picking up his pencil to do his math, he was shown the videotape of a day when he was more successful. Some days, he watched the video clip 1-2 times. He could then access the movement needed to do his math. On other days, he watched the video many times and still wasn't able to access his motor skills. However, overall, he became more fluid and consistent with his ability to do math. His relationships with his staff also improved, once they understood an effective way to support him.

Considerations: Video can be used to "pre-teach" before instruction actually occurs, thus providing the "picture" of what the instruction is going to look like prior to the task being started. This can assist individuals for whom making transitions is difficult.

EXAMPLES: **Logging on to the computer**

> "Filtering the geeky genes out of high-tech breeding grounds like Silicon Valley, in other words, might remove the very DNA that made these places what they are today." (Nash and Bonesteel 2002)

Goal: To teach the skill of logging on to the computer.

Implementation: Do a task analysis and then storyboard the steps involved in logging onto the computer. For example: turn on computer; wait for login box to appear; locate username box; using mouse, log on to home screen typing in user name; click "enter"; locate password box; using mouse, log on to home screen typing in password; click "enter"; as home screen appears, navigate to designated icon. Videotape and show the sequence to learner before they use the computer.

Considerations: Remember to consider the rules around being on the computer. Obtain the necessary passwords. Examine the angle from which you are shooting the video. It may be difficult to see the computer screen when filming head-on. If you want to include it as part of your shot, film the computer screen from a side angle.

EXAMPLES: **Pencil paper tasks**

> "Writing can be a major source of tension and struggle for students with autism. Some students cannot write at all and others, who can write, may have a difficult time doing so. Handwriting may be sloppy or even illegible. Students who struggle with writing may become frustrated with the

> process and become turned off to paper/pencil tasks. In order to support a student struggling with writing, a teacher may try to give the child gentle encouragement as he or she attempts to do some writing—a word, a sentence, or a few lines. Teachers might also allow the student to use a computer, word processor, or even an old typewriter for some lessons. In addition, peers, classroom volunteers, teachers, and paraprofessionals can also serve as scribes for a student who struggles with movement and motor problems, dictating as the student with autism speaks ideas and thoughts." (Kluth 2005)

Goal: To teach paper/pencil academic tasks in a manner that is consistent, clear and motivating.

Implementation: Set up materials in an area free of other visual stimuli. Videotape process with another individual completing the task.

Considerations: It will be necessary to determine the color of paper used (e.g., white paper vs. pastel paper). Some individuals with autism have noted that stark white paper can be a sensory irritant; for them, a specific pastel colored paper might be easier for the sensory system. An autistic individual once likened the sensation of looking at white paper to "needles poking my eyes." Another aspect to consider is the amount of print on the page or the number of problems to complete, as an entire worksheet of problems can be overwhelming. Identifying the number of problems to complete and visually marking them prior to the initiation of the task can be helpful. It can be helpful to analyze the amount of handwriting involved in a task and discern if there is a way to decrease it prior to the task being presented to the person. Seating options can be considered in a way that decreases extra stimuli and possibly seats the person as close to a written model as possible. Having a variety of ways for an individual to demonstrate work is helpful.

EXAMPLES: Reading a paragraph and answering questions

> "In the past I used to ask the same question over and over and I used to drive my parents crazy by doing that! I wanted to hear the same answer over and over because I was never sure of anything... I wanted an exact answer to everything; uncertainty used to drive me crazy." (McDonnell 1993)

Goal: To teach an individual to read a paragraph and answer questions in a manner that is consistent, clear and motivating.

Implementation: First, present material for the individual to read. Considerations around content and reading level need to be made. Readers may choose to read aloud. Once a passage has been read, have the individual complete a worksheet with questions. Questions may be answered in oral or written form. Videotape the process of reading a paragraph and answering the correlating questions.

A young adult with autism was decoding at a very high level but was not able to demonstrate comprehension of what he was reading. Judy Endow, autism consultant, theorized that he had not learned to make pictures in his head of what he was reading, once his reading got to a higher level. At early reading levels, pictures are often supplied. Then, as the reading levels go up, fewer and fewer pictures are supplied for the text. Thus, he could not demonstrate comprehension abilities at his higher decoding levels. Judy suggested he watch closed-circuit TV, as the dialogue is in writing and the context is supplied with pictures. He did so over the summer and it greatly increased his comprehension abilities.

Considerations: Make certain that the level of the reading material is commensurate with the individual's ability level. The presentation of the materials is important to some individuals' success. For instance, the format in which the questions are posed (e.g., fill-in format; "WH" questions, comment, multiple choice, etc.) can make the difference between competence being demonstrated or not. Verbal presentation might be more difficult for some individuals, who prefer to demonstrate their skills via written/visual choices. Some specific accommodations might need to be made such as changing the font for someone who finds using a larger font size when reading is optimal.

EXAMPLES: **Doing puzzles**

> "I felt secure in 'my world' and hated anything that tried to call me out of there... People, no matter how good, had no chance to compete." (Williams 1994)

Goal: To teach putting together puzzles in a manner that is consistent, clear and motivating.

Implementation: Set up materials in an area free of other visual stimuli. Videotape the process of putting together a puzzle with another individual completing the task.

For an individual learning to complete inset or non-inset puzzles, creating an outline of the puzzle can be helpful. By placing the completed puzzle on paper and removing one piece at a time, an outline can be made of the empty space on the paper using a black marker. As you remove each puzzle piece write a number on the back of the piece. In order for the puzzle pieces to correspond, also write the number on the paper in the spot where the piece will be correctly placed. Once completed with all pieces, laminate the paper and place it in the play area with the puzzle pieces in a small bin or basket. The individual can then complete the puzzle by matching the numbers or use the additional visual cues of the shapes outlined.

Considerations: Location (at table, desk or on floor) is important for some individuals when teaching this task. If the individual has difficulty with body mechanics, the floor may be a more appropriate place for instruction rather than a table or desk. For some, starting with a few pieces of the puzzle and covering the rest of the puzzle may be beneficial. Consider starting with single inset puzzles vs. interlocking puzzles. High interest themes can encourage participation in an activity. Puzzle themes such as *Thomas the Tank Engine* or *Star Wars* can increase interest and participation for some. Use the individual's passions. Depending on the individual you may wish to teach the routine from start to finish (getting puzzle from shelf or designated area within classroom and taking to the table).

EXAMPLES: Working in groups

> "I have trouble seeing the forest because the trees are so interesting. What I now realize is that I think 'backwards' from you guys. In college I took brilliant notes. I got so hung up with details I couldn't record the major ideas in a lecture because I just had to capture the lecturer's examples and details." (Roger N. Meyer in Ariel and Naseef 2006)

Goal: To teach individuals to work in group settings.

Implementation: Whether the group is academic or socially-based, establish the number of people within the group. Initially, a smaller group may be optimal. Identify individual roles of each group member. It may be helpful to identify the roles as task-oriented roles or process-oriented roles. For example, the process-oriented participants may ask key questions, encourage others, get things going, or make sure everyone is clear about what needs to be done. The task-oriented participants may initiate, clarify, take notes and summarize information. Develop PowerPoint slides to outline the steps.

Considerations: Working in a group setting can be a daunting task for individuals with autism. Identifying their role, being able to advocate in the process and completing the activity within the allotted time frame may be challenging. Visual supports may be appropriate to help assist the individual. Additional supports may be needed such as: index cards with identified roles on them; a talking stick to indicate who is talking and who should listen; timelines to support when work should be completed and by whom; graphic organizers outlining pertinent information to the task.

Developing "social scripts" ahead of time may be helpful for an individual who wishes to advocate their needs when in the group. If they have an additional idea or a different opinion than the rest of the group, having the wording easily available and accessible via a script may be beneficial.

EXAMPLES: Participation in science lab

> "I was rarely able to hear sentences because my hearing distorted them. I was sometimes able to hear a word or two at the start and understand it and then the next lot of words sort of merged into one another and I could not make head or tail of it." (Darren White in Cohen 1987)

Goal: To maximize participation in the science lab.

Implementation: Do a task analysis and storyboard the steps involved for participating in a specific science lab. Videotape each step for the individual to watch prior to entering the lab. Emphasize safety.

Considerations: Develop a supplemental video or PowerPoint presentation outlining the awareness of safety rules in the lab. Break down multi-step instructions by using a visual schedule within a schedule (mini-schedule). When choosing a lab partner for the individual, consider compatibility and relationships that they have already formed. Interpretation of marginal results (making estimations and/or approximations) may need further explanation and/or support. When lab results do not come out as expected, supporting the individual may be important. Using an iPod Touch with pre-loaded calming strategies and techniques is an option. Consider sensory sensitivities within a science lab: smell sensitivities (chemicals), auditory sensitivities (combustible experiments), tactile sensitivities (wearing safety glasses, gloves). Resource: Paula Kluth's website paulakluth.com; reference to "Adaptations for Participation in the Science Lab."

EXAMPLES: Study hall

> "Things are not always what they seem. I sometimes feel as if I am the eighth wonder of the world as people stare and marvel at my irregular behaviors, which lead to the poor assumption that I am simply mentally disabled with little or no intellectual functioning. My appearance is very deceptive..." (Sue Rubin in Biklen 2005)

Goal: To teach participation in a study hall that is functional as well as social, in a manner that is consistent, clear and motivating.

Implementation: Identify individual components that will promote optimal success (e.g., asking a teacher for help; asking a peer for help; seeking clarification; asking to go to a quieter location, etc.). Create a PowerPoint using pictures of the steps involved with each identified component. Add words, audio cues or narration. Show the PowerPoint presentation prior to the individual going to study hall.

Considerations: Support using organizational tools: iPod Touch, iPad or Palm Pilot for calendar and homework deadlines. Use visuals to prioritize work (i.e., timelines; graphic organizers). Practice routines on how to ask for help and support with visual aides such as reminder cards or mini-schedules.

EXAMPLES: Music class

> "I can do nothing alone ... I can do anything with ... I cannot initiate, but I can fully share." (Sacks 1990)

Goal: To increase participation in school specials as part of the general education curriculum.

Implementation: Create a PowerPoint of the sequence of steps involved with each activity within the music class. Add words, audio cues or narration. Prior to attending class, have the individual watch the PowerPoint.

Jose is a second-grade student with autism who loves music. Through the use of video modeling Jose was able to participate in class with his peers. He learned all of the necessary routines around using instruments, learning songs with actions, and beginning and ending routines for class. When it was time for the holiday performance, Jose's teachers showed him videos of performances from past years. They practiced standing on the risers, singing, entering and leaving the auditorium and taking a bow at the end of the performance. Jose successfully participated in the performance alongside his peers without any assistance. He received a standing ovation.

Considerations: Obtain lesson plans ahead of time from the music teacher so that preparation is accurate for each class. Different activities may trigger different sensory sensitivities. Include any sensory strategies in the PowerPoint, e.g., noise-reduction devices such as earplugs or headphones.

EXAMPLES: **Changing into gym clothes**

> "Puberty arrived when I was 14 years old, and nerve attacks accompanied it. I started living in a constant state of stage fright, the way you feel before your first big job interview or public speaking engagement. But in my case, the anxiety seized me for no good reason." (Grandin in Baron et al. 2006)

Goal: To assist the individual in maximizing their independence by acquiring self-care skills such as changing into their gym clothes.

Implementation: Storyboard the steps involved. Videotape the locker room routine and show it to the individual prior to gym class.

Considerations: Determine the location of gym clothes (i.e., in gym bag vs. locker). Discern the individual's sensory sensitivities that might be affected during this skill sequence (e.g., odors, fluorescent lighting, echoing, general noise level). It may be helpful to determine if the time allotted for the class to change will be enough for the individual or if more time will be necessary. Some specifics of time-savers are aspects such as: tie-shoes vs. Velcro shoes; fine motor skills necessary to change clothing; who will provide assistance if needed. One consideration, especially for older individuals is to make certain there is a same-sex staff person available for assistance if needed. Also, it might be important for some people to do an assessment of environmental safety concerns (e.g., wet floors).

EXAMPLES: **Physical education**

Goal: Increase independence and participation in physical education class.

Implementation: Videotape the current and/or upcoming unit and have the individual watch the video prior to participation in the targeted activity. Use visuals to support steps. Units may need to be broken down into steps and taught piecemeal.

Tony is a high school student with autism. When his physical education class changed activities, it often took him several weeks to catch on to the new activity, and that left him behind his peers. He was given the opportunity to videotape each new activity when the PE class started a new unit, and watch it at home and during study halls. This greatly assisted him in being able to keep up with his classmates and access the necessary skills.

Considerations: Some individuals prefer to watch a new routine or activity and then join in when comfortable. Allowing for this processing time may assist in participation in the activity. Sports activities which have a high energy level and complex steps in execution can be overwhelming to a person's sensory and learning system. Consider which parts of an activity and at what level participation can be individualized. Think about team vs. individual sports (individual sports are often easier for autistic individuals to engage). Consider having a location in the gymnasium for the individual to complete specified routines if they are unable to participate fully in the activity at hand.

EXAMPLES: **Recess routine**

> "They told me I would have friends but the playground was a nightmare of noise and fighting, lying, and cheating and people going fast, all knowing what to do but me. It was like a flock of birds, wheeling, surging, changing direction at a whim, all knowing what to do, and all in unison except for one at the back. Me. I had to watch and anticipate and follow so I was never quite in harmony. Sometimes I got left behind and there are hawks out there. I didn't know how to tell who was a friend." (Geraldine Robertson in Attwood 2009)

Goal: To increase participation in social environments (e.g., playground) with peers

Implementation: Inventory the skills that the individual's peers play most frequently on the playground. Take pictures of each playground activity and have the individual choose which skills they would like to learn to play with friends at recess.

Videotape the activity/activities the individual has chosen in the environment where it will occur on the playground.

Considerations: One aspect that is particularly important to consider with the playground is sensory sensitivities: auditory (e.g., number of individuals on the playground, noise levels); visual (e.g., movement of individuals on the playground, clothing types); tactile (e.g., wood chips, playground equipment, sand, temperature and wind); olfactory (e.g., outside air, perspiration of peers). Some questions to discern might be: Which playground sub environment is optimal for social interaction? What types of activities does the individual prefer? Will the preferred activity work better in a small group vs. large group? What is the best location of play that may allow for the most consistency and availability on a regular basis? A student will require a completely different video for indoor recess vs. outdoor recess since the activity choices are differant. The student may enjoy shooting the video (perhaps with assistance). Filming it themselves may heighten others' awareness of the student's interest in the game they are playing. In addition, it may offer an opportunity for the individual to observe the game/activity in the course of creating the video.

EXAMPLES: Using the water fountain/bubbler

> "It is known that sometimes people with autism have trouble moving their bodies. This is known as motor planning inability. Sometimes I have trouble making my body do what I want it to do." (Jamie Burke)

Goal: To maximize independence within the context of functional routines, such as using the water fountain/bubbler in school and/or in the community.

Implementation: Storyboard the steps involved. Videotape the environment (location of water fountain in hallway or locker room) and routine for using the water fountain. Show the video to the individual prior to going to the hallway for a drink.

Considerations: There are some related skills that need to be considered with this skill, such as: waiting your turn in line; what to do if someone has used the water fountain before you inappropriately; when to use the water fountain (between classes, on a break from class, on the way to lunch, etc.). In addition, there are some personal preferences and abilities that need to be considered, such as: tactile sensitivities; fine motor skills necessary to operate the water fountain; proximity of mouth to the bubbler; preparing for the varied temperature of the water in different fountains. This skill lends itself to having the video or PowerPoint loaded onto a handheld electronic device (e.g., MP3 player, iPod Touch, iPad) so the individual can have easy access to the video technology whenever necessary.

EXAMPLES: Lunchroom routine

> "I have just come from another classroom where I had been tortured by sharp white fluorescent light, which made reflections bounce off everything. It made the room race busily in a constant state of change. Light and shadow dancing on people's faces as they spoke turned the scene into an animated cartoon." (Williams 1994)

Goal: To maximize independence within a social environment, completing a daily living skill such as a lunchroom routine.

Implementation: Do a task analysis and storyboard the steps involved, for instance: obtain the lunch tray; obtain necessary utensils and napkin; walk through the line, select preferred food items and place them on the tray; push tray through the line; pay for food/use lunch ticket or electronic system. It may also be beneficial in the video to include how the individual will select seating within the lunchroom setting.

Considerations: There are some related skills to consider including in the lunch video, such as: choosing cold lunch vs. hot lunch; entering the lunchroom early when there are fewer people in the environment; using a visual script for ordering items in the cafeteria. Due to the bombardment of sensory stimuli in a cafeteria setting, considering the individual's sensory sensitivities is important in this environment. Some examples of what one might consider: auditory (e.g., noise level in cafeteria, noise level made by chewing different foods); smell (e.g., food and closeness of peers when sitting at tables and in line); tactile (texture of food, hot vs. cold); visual (e.g., lighting, people). Additional supports may be taught as part of the lunch routine, such as a mini-schedule and a system for previewing the menu and making choices ahead of time. An assessment may need to be conducted to determine if the individual has the fine motor skills necessary to use utensils, wipe their mouth with a napkin, as well as the movement capacity to eat at a moderated pace. If there are needs in these areas, supports could be built into the video.

EXAMPLES: Homework

> "A daily homework timetable can be made by a parent with guidance from the teacher to define the expected duration and content of each homework activity or assignment. This can be extremely helpful if there are prob-

lems with the child's allocation of time to each homework component. Sometimes the homework can take hours when the teacher intended only several minutes on a specified task." (Attwood 2000)

Goal: To maximize independence within the context of functional routines, by learning a homework routine.

Implementation: A PowerPoint presentation of the individualized steps and routines around homework may be useful. Have the individual watch the steps prior to starting their homework.

Considerations: Even with a homework routine in place, it may be necessary to negotiate with the teacher as to the amount of homework a student is expected to do. For many students with ASD, it is useful to decrease the overall amount of homework, since it may take even the brightest student with ASD exponentially longer to complete the same amount of work as it might take a neurotypical peer. As individuals get older it is important to teach the skill of looking at a task/assignment and breaking it down into manageable components, which are then placed on a timeline. It is helpful if this is done systematically (i.e, the support team and family use the same approach which is agreed upon ahead of time). Initially, the process is completed for the individual in front of the individual, so they can observe the process repeatedly. Over time, they are taught to do portions of the skill sequence until eventually they are able to use the specific form or sequence to break down their own tasks.

Many schools require students to use an assignment notebook in which homework is noted for each day. Often a parent signature is necessary on a daily or weekly basis. If the student's school uses assignment notebooks, the sequence for how to use the notebook needs to be incorporated into the video. Some learners benefit from a visual timer when doing homework, which depicts how much time to spend on each task or on homework as a whole. However, for some learners, the presence of a visual timer adds undue stress to a homework situation that is possibly already anxiety producing. In these cases, it may be more helpful to designate a specific amount of work to be completed, rather than an amount of time.

Extracurricular

EXAMPLES: Girl Scouts

> "Ours is a circle of friendships united by ideals." (Juliette G. Low)

> "Like many autistic children, 8-year-old Magi Klages finds new situations to be stressful. So her parents weren't surprised when she began acting out by biting herself and running around at her first gathering with her new Girl Scout troop in Wisconsin earlier this month. But despite the fact that the troop she joined was specifically created for children with special needs, the troop leader decided that Magi was a 'danger' to the other children and promptly kicked her out of the troop." (Maple 2008)

Goal: Increase participation in extracurricular activities within the community and to increase social connections with peers via Girl Scouts. Note: Video technology can be used to increase social connections and participation in any extracurricular club or activity.

Implementation: Storyboard the steps involved in a typical club meeting. Videotape the targeted activity/routine within the Girl Scout meeting. Identify the place and time for instruction as well as peer models. Identify the instructional cue to begin the task if necessary.

Considerations: Preparing individuals for the structure and routines within a monthly meeting setting or at a community event can be very helpful. Some situations that may be useful are: videotape routines for the opening and closing ceremonies at Girl Scout meetings; pre-teach activities for meetings by videotaping elements involved in earning badges; videotape routines/environments for community-based outings (camp, movie day, parades, etc.).

EXAMPLES: Drama

> "I made mistakes in drama. I thought drama was when actors cried. But drama is when the audience cries." (Frank Capra)

Goal: To increase participation in extracurricular activities and social participation with peers via drama.

Implementation: Storyboard the steps involved in completing the play. Recognize the materials required for the task (e.g., props, materials, stage settings). Identify the place and time for instruction as well as peer models. Identify the instructional cue to begin the task if necessary. Videotape the sequence of steps for the targeted activity/routine within the drama club.

Andrea was a high school student with autism who was interested in drama. The high school drama club supervisor was looking for ways to include Andrea, who was nonverbal. The club supervisor approached her special education support teacher. Together with the help of Andrea's speech and language therapist, they programmed an iPod Touch, along with an amplification system (iMainGo), to deliver Andrea's two lines in the play. In addition, her team developed a PowerPoint presentation with photos of the parts that she would be in, which Andrea watched daily. In the beginning, she needed a support person to help prompt her when to use her Speak It! program to say her part but during the play rehearsal and performance, Andrea delivered her lines all by herself.

Considerations: Identify areas of interest within the drama club. For some individuals building sets and making costumes may be of high interest. For others, acting may be preferred. Consider sensory sensitivities to sound, sight and smells. The bright lights of a stage performance as well as flash bulbs from cameras can often have a long lasting effect on an individual with autism.

EXAMPLES: **Chess club**

> "Everyone would be asked to join all clubs if desired and pleasing music would play everywhere." (Jamie Burke)

Goal: Increase participation in extracurricular activities and increase social participation with peers via chess club. Provide opportunities for participation in high interest activities.

Implementation: May need to pre-teach aspects of playing the game of chess, such as: recognize the materials required (chess pieces, board, timer); identify the place and time for instruction, etc. Before making a PowerPoint or video of chess play, it may be helpful to create a task analysis of the steps required to set up and play the game. Add words, audio cues or narration.

Demetri, a middle-school student with autism, is an avid chess player. He learned early and played often with his dad. As Demetri grew older and became a savvy Internet user, he continued to learn chess strategy and tactics through online videos at various sites such as YouTube, KebuChess.com and Chess.com/videos. Demetri's father now reports that he is no match for his thirteen-year-old son!

Considerations: Team competitions often have different rules than individual matches. Supporting the individual with a visual highlighting "same vs. different" within the context of an individual match and team competition may be useful. Consider videotaping the process for what to do when you are waiting your turn to play, competition, rules of the game, and sportsmanship. For some individuals, it is necessary to have one video for when they win in chess and a separate one for when they lose, so they can access the sportsmanship behaviors involved in each scenario (e.g., shaking hands, saying "nice match," congratulating winner, and accessing graciousness when losing or winning).

EXAMPLES: **Academic bowls**

> "He told me that his teachers reported that ... he was mentally slow, unsociable, and adrift forever in his foolish dreams." (Hans Albert Einstein, on his father, Albert Einstein)

Goal: To increase participation in extracurricular activities and social participation with their peers. To provide opportunities for individuals to demonstrate their gifts and talents.

Implementation: Videotape the structure and format of the academic bowl. You may need to pre-teach individual components (e.g., how to ring-in if you know the answer; answer formats; where to stand; the order of events, etc.)

Martin, an academically talented high school student, enjoyed participating in academic bowls. While he often knew many of the answers, he and his team didn't usually place in the bowls because Martin wasn't able to hit the ringer fast enough to get a chance to answer the questions first. His team captain and staff coach noticed that when an opposing team had missed a question and the question was defaulted to Martin's team, he often knew the answer. To prepare for the next academic bowl, the team captain, Martin and the staff coach devised a plan whereby Martin would stand next to the team captain and poke him when he knew the answer. For some reason, poking his team captain was easier for Martin than ringing the buzzer. The team practiced this when they got together, videotaping Martin poking the team captain for each question to which he knew the answer. At the next bowl, Martin poked the team captain when questions were asked. Sometimes he even poked the captain before the question was asked, yet Martin consistently knew most of the answers. When the captain asked Martin about this, Martin replied, "When I know something, I tend to know everything about that category so you could save yourself a lot of poking by ringing in on all the questions in that category!"

Considerations: It will be important to consider the individual's sensory sensitivities as they relate to the environment in which the academic bowl will be held (e.g., sound, light, echoing of theater area, etc.). Also, be cautious that an individual may need to be equally prepared for each academic bowl, especially if the environments or rules change. Consider alternate response formats if the individual is having difficulty using a buzzer.

EXAMPLES: **Student council**

> "Jenny has taught me that even the smallest, most arcane detail—such as the light cover on a streetlight—is worth a look. Her questions and comments have forced me to think and to learn about much more in life than I otherwise would have." (Phil Dougherty in Ariel and Nareef 2006)

Goal: To increase participation in extracurricular activities and to promote social participation with peers via student council.

Implementation: Consider routines that are important to teach for increased participation at student council meetings. Videotape the routines and pre-teach these routines prior to the meetings. Videotape individual routines (e.g., opening and closing of the meeting, snack times, seating arrangements, etc.).

Considerations: Individuals may need visuals to support time and place (e.g., if after school, a visual to indicate when, where, and who will be picking up the individual may be useful). Develop "social scripts" ahead of time for the individual to advocate their needs when in the group. If an individual has an additional idea or has a different opinion than the rest of the group, have the wording accessible via a visual prompt. Consider having multiple forms of technology available through which individuals can comment, give ideas and participate in group activities. Have an AlphaSmart, iPad or computer on which to write out answers and to ask questions in a larger group setting.

EXAMPLES: **Homework club**

> "People are always looking for that single magic bullet that will totally change everything. There is no single magic bullet." (Grandin 1996)

Goal: To help support academic growth and to promote social participation with peers.

Implementation: Identify individual components that will promote optimal success, such as asking a teacher for help, asking a peer for help, seeking clarification, etc. Create a PowerPoint presentation using pictures of the sequence of steps involved with each identified component. You may want to add words to the actions at the bottom of the screen. Consider adding a voice to give an audio cue on each step. Show the presentation prior to the individual attending the homework club.

Austin, a junior high school student with Asperger's syndrome, struggled with time management during homework club. He would frequently forget what he needed to do for homework. Austin's case manager knew that Austin had an iPod Touch and recommended that they utilize an application called Visual Scheduler to track his homework and help him manage his time. Austin's parents helped him load the application onto his iPod. After minimal instruction, he now uses the application to program in his homework daily and put what materials he needs for each assignment. With the help of his teacher he also gauges how much time it will take him to complete each assignment so he can leave enough time for each subject area.

Considerations: It is also possible to target social skills that are not specific to homework, such as greetings and asking others what they are going to be doing later.

Consider including social scripts in the PowerPoint or video for homework club that would help the student understand when to apply the scripts. Determine ahead of time what things in homework club are variable and what things stay the same (e.g., the supervisor, the music, the group of students, location). For the things that are changeable, include in the PowerPoint as many of the possibilities that are viable to assist the student in generalizing.

EXAMPLES: **Prom**

> "Autism is not a puzzle, nor a disease. Autism is a challange [sic], but certainly not a devistating [sic] one. Autism is about having a pure heart and being very sensitive... It is about finding a way to survive in an overwhelming, confusing world... It is about developing differently, in a different pace and with different leaps. Autistic beings develop and bloom if their spirits, talents and self-esteem are not destroyed by bullies, preju-

dice, 'doggie-training,' and being forced to be 'normal.' " (Trisha Van Berkel)

Goal: To increase participation in extra curricular activities and promote social participation and inclusion with peers, via attending prom.

Implementation: Consider routines that are important to teach for increased participation at the prom: asking someone to go to prom; grooming (hair and/or nails, dress or suit); flowers; transportation; photographs; dancing lessons; going out to eat; going as a couple vs. going with a group of friends. Videotape the routines and pre-teach prior to the prom.

Considerations: The environment where prom will take place will of course vary from year to year (i.e., school vs. a community setting). One friend with autism has a sensory response to having her picture taken which results in her seeing flashes for hours after someone has taken a flash picture. This is the kind of sensory sensitivity that needs to be considered when preparing someone for the prom. For this person, it would be important to include a video clip of someone asking that flash photography not be used in her presence, just as one might ask for someone with a seizure disorder.

EXAMPLES: Going to a football game

"When is an obsession not an obsession? When it is football!" (Paula Kluth)

Goal: To increase participation in extra curricular activities and to increase social participation with peers and the community, via attending a football game of a local or school team.

Implementation: Identify specific routines that are necessary to teach, such as: seating (e.g., types, where to sit, etc.); outside vs. inside; clothing; peer support; food allergies and other sensitivities; knowledge of cheers. Include routines such as paying to get in and ordering/paying at the concession stand. Videotape the environment, including the location of where to enter the field, where to pay, finding a place to sit, concession stand, etc. Teach necessary routines by showing the video to the individual prior to going to the game.

Considerations: Consider sensory sensitivities to sound (e.g., crowd noise, sound of buzzer indicating start of game, end of quarter), lights, temperature/wind, smells from the concession stand, etc. Use visual scripts to assist with social aspects of game. Visually map out sections of the bleacher where the individual can sit. Develop a plan ahead of time for the individual to meet friends at the game.

EXAMPLES: Bowling

> "She looked at me and said, 'you know, Mr. Clark, you'll do fine. As long as you can affect the life of one child, you've been a success.' To this day I do not like that quote. I feel we have to approach education with the determination to affect each and every one of our individuals... I approach each year with the knowledge that I have only one year to make a life's worth of difference in each child in that classroom, and I give it everything I've got." (Ron Clark)

Goal: To increase participation in competitive sports either as an active participant or as a support to the team, via bowling.

Implementation: Storyboard the steps involved. Make a PowerPoint presentation using pictures of the sequence. Add words, audio cues or narration. Support the PowerPoint with a video of skills. It may also help to have the individual watch bowling on television. Show the PowerPoint presentation before bowling.

Considerations: Additional skills that are required in this setting include: securing bowling shoes; purchasing refreshments; scoring; locating and fitting a bowling ball; location of the restrooms. For each of the above areas, it would be helpful to conduct a task analysis and videotape the sequence, perhaps teaching one portion of it at a time. Some dimensions to consider when task analyzing these sequences, would be whether or not electronic or handwritten scoring would be used, and whether an individual will rent shoes and ball or use their own personal items.

As with all environments, it will be important to consider any sensory sensitivities the individual may have specific to the particular bowling alley that will be used. Some individuals may require a noise-blocking device such as headphones or earplugs, for instance, while others may benefit from a scented cloth to address olfactory sensitivities. Whatever the individual's needs, it is important to include the use of these accommodations into the video.

Some individuals who are new to bowling benefit from having bumpers in the gutters so that the ball doesn't repeatedly end up in the gutter. This allows an individual to learn scoring while also learning technique. If bumpers are used, it will be important to have videos both with and without the bumpers, so the individual has the support necessary to change the internal picture of bowling with bumpers to bowling without them.

For most individuals learning to bowl, it is helpful to have a routine connected to releasing the ball. For instance, a person may start at the same spot on the alley, take three steps and release the ball as they bend down on the fourth step. It might be useful to have the printed directions for the sequence added to the videotape (i.e., start at the mark; take three steps: 1, 2, 3; bend down and release the ball). It may be helpful for the individual to play bowling on the Wii or another such video game, as this could potentially strengthen their understanding of the game, scoring, etc.

EXAMPLES: Tennis

> "Children's reactions to their own physical [differences] are largely a reflection of the way they have been treated by others." (Hallahan and Kauffman 1993)

Goal: To increase participation in competitive sports either as an active participant or as a support to the team, via tennis.

Implementation: Videotape individual strokes for the individual to learn before playing tennis. Once individual skills are mastered, you can videotape a tennis match and highlight the individual components. Video examples of how scoring works may be also useful.

Emily, a high school sophomore with autism, was interested in learning how to play tennis. She had already been successful in the school setting using visual supports in the form of schedules and social scripts. Emily's teacher decided to pre-teach many of the tennis strokes by videotaping them being done by some of her peers. They demonstrated each swing, backhand, forehand, etc. Emily watched the video of her peers demonstrating the swings and then also playing the game of tennis. Prior to physical education class, she would watch the videos on the computer in her classroom. When on the tennis court, Emily also had the video's loaded onto her iPod Touch and would frequently watch the videos between sets. Her mother reported that Emily also watched the videos at home. Emily not only learned the sport, but also joined the tennis team at her high school as a manager the first year and then as a team member.

Considerations: Think about the individual's familiarity with the sport. Consider whether it is an individual vs. team activity. Many autistic individuals report increased success in individualized sports. It may be helpful to have the individual play tennis on the Wii Sports or another such video game, to support their understanding of the game and scoring, as well as providing a "picture" of what tennis looks like when being played. Another alternative to this would be having the student watch a tennis match on television, pointing out the strategies, strokes, and highlighting the key elements of the game.

EXAMPLES: Basketball

> "It's not so much about winning or losing, but the process, and being able to participate." (Jerry Newport 1999)

Goal: To increase participation in competitive sports either as an active participant or as a support to the team, via basketball.

Implementation: When teaching competitive sports like basketball to individuals, it is often helpful to work on one skill at a time, such as dribbling or passing, then rebounding and, finally, running a play. Videotape each skill in practice and present the information to the individual. As they progress through each skill, you may want to put some of the skills together by splicing them into a continuous stream (e.g., dribbling and passing together). Continue to add skills for a complete presentation. Once separate skills are mastered, videotape working as a team, running plays and playing defense. Highlight how scoring works (2-point plays, 3-point shots, free-throws).

Considerations: It will be necessary to inventory the individual's gross motor skill level involved with each sport. Sensory sensitivities will also need assessment and accommodation, such as: auditory (e.g., echoing of noise in gymnasium); visual (e.g., movement of other individuals, lighting in gymnasium, sound of equipment hitting the floor). One person may need sunglasses or a visor to block fluorescent lights, while another may need an auditory blocking device (e.g., earplugs, headphones) due to sensitivity to the echoing of noise in a gymnasium or the sound of the equipment hitting the floor. It may be helpful to teach the drills individually and slowly move into doing them with the team. It may be helpful to have the individual watch basketball on television or play it on Wii Sports or other video games, to strengthen their understanding of the game.

Once there is an overall understanding of the game, a level of participation can be considered on an individual basis. For instance, one individual may learn several positions while another may only learn defense or one particular position, such as point guard. It might provide a nice succession of skills to start out with individual drills and move into team drills before moving into team play of basketball.

EXAMPLES: Using the Wii

> "Until we had the Wii the 2 of them never shared let alone play a game together and actually take turns. The Wii has taught him turn taking and makes it easy for him to play a game with someone else instead of always by himself." (Bonnie Sayers, Bella Online Autism Spectrum Disorders Editor)

Goal: To increase participation in competitive sports either as an active participant or as a support to the team, using the Wii video gaming system.

Implementation: Within the Wii system there are training modules that teach games such as tennis and bowling and track progress. The interactive hand controller has a virtual-reality aspect that allows the on-screen figure to mimic the motions made by your arm. Supplement by videotaping a sibling/peer playing the games.

Sam, a young man with autism, was interested in purchasing a Wii, but wanted to learn more about it before obtaining one himself. My then 11-year-old son, Augie, had a Wii, so I asked him to set it up for me before school on the days I was seeing Sam. One day I forgot to ask Augie to set it up, which caused great disappointment for Sam. I asked my son to write out the rather convoluted steps for connecting the Wii to our outdated home entertainment equipment. The next time Sam arrived, I showed him the directions and we set it up together, with him taking a lead. The very next time Sam came for a session, I had misplaced the directions. I said, "I'm so sorry that we won't be able to use the Wii today, as I've misplaced the directions." Sam replied that he no longer needed the directions, since he'd set it up once and remembered the steps. (However, I myself still need the directions these several years later.)

Considerations: For some individuals, it is helpful to master a certain game before adding additional players. Others might prefer to have at least one other person involved in the two-person games from the beginning, so that the routine of playing doesn't have to be changed once it's learned. Sometimes video games can trigger sensory and movement differences. In the Wii Fit Plus, for example, there are some balance exercises that require using a 2 ft. x 3 ft. platform which is placed on the floor. One autistic person was unable to participate in balancing because her sensory issues with dizziness and vertigo precluded her ability to balance on the board.

In the community

EXAMPLES: Community functioning

> "Our people don't want to spend all sixty or more years of adult life in the first situation they go into when they leave home!" (Newport and Newport 2002)

Goal: The individual will be able to perform independently in the community environments related to activities of daily living (ADLs).

Implementation: Videotape or take digital photos of the community environment of highest priority for the individual. Assess the environment in regards to: preparation (e.g., getting wallet, writing/typing shopping list, etc.); transportation; foyers/vestibules/stairway; entrance; pattern for accessing the environment; the actual sequence; leave-taking; follow up (e.g., groceries put away, wallet back in drawer, etc.). Show the video prior to accessing the environment.

Considerations: It may be helpful to have a person performing the skill sequence in the environment exactly the way the individual will be taught. For instance, if they are going to be taught to use a picture-coded shopping list and calculator, have a person modeling that in the video. If using digital photos, one could create a sequence of slides for a PowerPoint presentation. Write a social story for the sequence, one sentence for each photo. Have the individual view the presentation prior to going to the community environment. For further support, have them or another person record reading the words for each photo and add the audio to the slides. If a portable device is preferred, the same kind of story can be created on the StoryMaker application for the iPod Touch, and the individual could then bring the device to the store to view as they shopped.

EXAMPLES: Grocery shopping

> "You have got to keep autistic children engaged with the world. You cannot let them tune out." (Grandin 1996)

Goal: To teach grocery shopping in the natural environment.

Implementation: Storyboard the steps involved. A sequence of steps might run as follows: walks/ambulates to store's entrance (from transportation); scans for/determines "in" door; opens "in" door or waits for door to open (if automatic); ambulates through door; scans for cart; obtains cart; places shopping list and calculator in the cart rack; scans for first item on the shopping list; ambulates through store, scanning for initial item on the list; stops when item is located; picks up item and places it in the cart; continues until all items are in the cart; scans for check out; ambulates to check out; scans for shortest check out line; ambulates to shortest check out line; places grocery items on the counter or conveyor; responds to cashier's questions and social repartee; obtains money from purse or wallet; pays for groceries upon natural cue from cashier or monitor display; waits for/obtains change; places change in purse/wallet; picks up grocery bag; scans for "out" door; ambulates to "out" door; puts cart away; ambulates to transportation.

Videotape a person grocery shopping in the sequence that will be taught to the individual. Have the individual watch the videotape prior to grocery shopping.

One young woman with autism was videotaped grocery shopping and riding a city bus when she was in high school. Now, fifteen years later, she is experiencing some difficulties accessing movement as fluidly as she did when she was a teenager. This "old" video of her can be shown to her now, before going in the community. Seeing the video may facilitate her ability to access more fluid movement. Watching the video with staff may help in their understanding of her current frustration. The video provides a kind of historical record and point of reference to share with others, including those who specialize in understanding movement differences and diversity, who might be able to provide some additional ideas of supporting and accommodating for her in her present situation.

Considerations: Arrange the video in titled sections: Entrance; Locating items; Checkout; Leaving. Download the segments onto a handheld electronic device such as an iPod Touch or iPad, or create it using an application designed for the device, so the individual can watch a segment immediately prior to executing that portion of the grocery-shopping sequence.

EXAMPLES: Airports

"When you add to the mix the possibility of a complete physical frisk or pat down—and the presence and scrutiny of armed, uniformed paramilitary personnel and contraband-sniffing dogs—the accompanying sensory-enhancing gauntlet of sounds, lights and touch can tax the system of any traveler let alone one who has autism. This experience has quickly become standard operating procedure at U.S. airports." (Debbaudt 2001)

Goal: To assist individuals in processing and preparing for the experience of traveling on an airplane.

Implementation: It is difficult to find videos of airports that display what the experience is truly like. Most movie clips are either in the comedic or action-adventure realms and are not exactly accurate portrayals. Fortunately, the U.S. Transportation Security Administration has made a series of videos that can help prepare children for airport travel. These videos show people the entire experience of going to the airport, including what happens when going through security checkpoints (removal of liquids from your bag, taking off your shoes, how to go through metal detector, etc.). You can watch these videos with the individual before you go on the trip. The website is: http://www.tsa.gov/travelers/airtravel/children/.

Considerations: For individuals that can read maps, it may be beneficial to have copies of airport maps for the specific airports that you will be visiting. Individuals can study the maps before they leave, and if they know gate assignments ahead of time, can even map out the best routes to take within the airport.

EXAMPLES: Street crossing

"I don't hand hold, but I'm a good lantern." (Donna Williams)

Goal: Crossing the street safely.

Implementation: Storyboard the steps involved. Have someone cross the street in the manner the individual will be taught to do. Have them watch the video prior to going in the community.

Considerations: Include as many variations of street crossings as possible, such as those with and without walk/don't walk signals; different speed zones; those with and without marked crosswalks; crossing from an intersection versus the middle of the street; crossing in a quiet neighborhood versus a busy intersection, etc.

It might be helpful to include some kind of concrete cue for a person to assist in making the judgment about crossing the street. For some, it is best to have the rule be "no moving car in sight." Other individuals prefer to learn to watch from a particular point a certain measured distance away and count seconds. For one person, tape was put on the street and he was taught that he could not cross if a car was closer to him than the tape. Due to his strong visual abilities, he was able to generalize that distance to other street crossing situations and the tape was not necessary once he "internalized" the distance that was depicted initially by the tape. The distance was made far enough away that it took into account varying speeds of cars.

EXAMPLES: Stopping when someone says "stop"

> "I had no idea why anyone did anything but I knew if someone was 'real,' when a fight was coming, whether others were trying to invade 'my world.' My senses and perception were chaotic, fragmented and constantly shifting and fluctuating and the ability to understand things with meaning was so delayed I looked like I wasn't 'on line' but also like someone very behaviorally and emotionally disturbed." (Donna Williams)

> "Tragically, children and adults with autism are often attracted to water sources such as pools, ponds, and lakes. Drowning is a leading cause of death for a child or adult who has autism." (Dennis Debbaudt, National Autism Association 2005)

Goal: To improve safety skills.

Implementation: When individuals with autism run away from a parent/provider, whether it is in a safe, enclosed area or one that is open, it can lead to danger. Many safety concerns present themselves in this situation. It will be important when teaching this skill initially, that you do so within the context of an already established routine. Videotape a sequence of start/stop opportunities. Reinforce successful trials.

Considerations: Videotape the student stopping on cue in a variety of situations/settings. Use discrete trial format/applied behavior analysis (see glossary) with two people: one to say stop and the other to prompt them to stop on cue. It is helpful when using discrete trial to do many successive trials at a time so that the behavior becomes ingrained. Have the individual watch a videotape of the discrete trial sessions initially because it will give them a picture of stopping when they are cued to stop. Begin in a more protected area and then only when the student is demonstrating the skill successfully, move into more chaotic, busier community environments.

EXAMPLES: Calling 911

> "I lived in an emotional and perceptual chaos which taught me surrealism and the relativity of the word 'normal' for there are many different versions of 'normality.' I was nine before I could fluently understand with meaning three sentences in a row, was largely meaning deaf and meaning blind as well as face-blind but learned to map pattern and feel shifts and changes with remarkable ability in spite of pretty much no ability to interpret." (Donna Williams)

Goal: To improve safety awareness.

Implementation: Calling for help when it is needed is essential for overall independence. Identifying situations that require 911assistance is also critical. Identify the sequence of steps that will promote optimal success: locating phone; listening for a dial tone; dialing 911; stating your name and address; identifying what help is needed, etc. Create a PowerPoint presentation using pictures of the subsequent steps involved with each identified component. Add text or audio cues. Show the PowerPoint presentation prior to a model of the emergency.

Considerations: Have visual support or ID to provide information to 911 operators. It can also be helpful to assess the prerequisite phone skills necessary to use the phone. If the individual does not possess phone skills, teach them using video technology prior to teaching safety awareness of calling 911. Finally, a list

911 i.d. sheet

My name is: ______________________________

My address is: ______________________________

Parents' names ______________________________

I need help because: ______________________________

of valid "911 emergencies" may need to be listed somewhere near the telephone. One individual with autism called 911 when he ran out of dish detergent, because, to him, this constituted an emergency.

EXAMPLES: **Wearing a seatbelt**

> "Whatever the reasons, I, as an autistic person, reacted in a fixated behavior pattern in order to reduce arousal to my over-stimulated nervous system." (Grandin 1986)

Goal: To promote safety awareness via wearing a safety belt.

Implementation: Do a task analysis and storyboard the steps involved. For example: grasp the shoulder strap with hand; pull strap across body; grasp the insert part of the belt with the other hand; locate stationary end of the buckle (i.e., "female" portion of the buckle); insert shoulder strap buckle (i.e., "male" portion of the buckle) into stationary end. Take pictures of individual steps of the process and insert into a PowerPoint presentation or the StoryMaker application for iPod Touch, adding voice to the steps if desired. Prior to getting into the car, show the sequence to the individual. Supplement with video of process.

Considerations: Consider varying vehicles (e.g., school bus, parent's car, friend's car) to promote generalization of skill. For some individuals, each type of seatbelt (e.g., lap belt, shoulder/lap belt) may need a separate video support; for others, the generalization will occur with just one type of seatbelt depicted. Inventory the necessary motor skills for using a seatbelt prior to implementation of this video or PowerPoint teaching.

EXAMPLES: **Elevator behavior**

> "When I encounter a new social situation, I have to scan my memory and look for previous experiences that were similar. As I accumulate more memories, I become more and more skilled at predicting how other people will act in a particular situation." (Grandin 1995)

Goal: To increase understanding of the "unwritten social rules and expectations of behavior that we all seem to know, but were never taught" (Bieber 1994).

Implementation: Set up PowerPoint slides for review. Take pictures of each step: getting onto the elevator; identifying where to stand in the elevator; pushing button for your floor or asking someone else to do so; conversation and comments that are appropriate for setting (may want to use conversation bubbles for this); exiting the elevator at your location. Prior to accessing the elevator, review pictures and practice scenarios. Supplement the PowerPoint presentation with a video of the entire sequence.

Jeremy, an eighth-grade student with Asperger's, was looking at the 2010 *Hidden Curriculum One-A-Day Calendar for Older Adolescents and Adults: Items for Understanding Unstated Rules in Social Situations* by Judy Endow, in the school psychologist's office. As he turned to the date, which addressed a tip on appropriate elevator behavior, Jeremy replied that he "never knew that that is what you are supposed to do in an elevator." He continued reading the tip and remarked that he thought he needed more help on learning "these things" because there were many he did not know. In Jeremy's sessions with his speech and language therapist, they began practicing the appropriate elevator behavior routines and also practiced the behaviors within the community. Jeremy utilized video modeling as a strategy to learn the appropriate elevator behavior.

Considerations: Add text or audio cues for each step of the PowerPoint presentation. May want to include different types of elevators in the video, such as typical vs. glass, making note that whatever the elevator looks like, "elevator behavior" remains the same.

EXAMPLES: Job interview skills

> "Aside from the inherent social challenges, I believe the most critical challenge for young adults with autism is finding and keeping jobs that are commensurate with each individual's true potential and area of interest. This is true even for those autistic adults who successfully complete a college degree." (Carolyn Komich Hare, MS, founder and director of AHEADD, Achieving in Higher Education With Autism/Developmental Disabilities)

Goal: To increase employability skills through teaching interview skills.

Implementation: Individuals with autism often have difficulty accessing their skills in new or unfamiliar situations like job interviews. Visual technology can be a way not only to practice the necessary skills needed in an interview setting, but also may provide a means for individuals to "showcase" their skills. Identify through a task analysis the necessary components/steps of skills needed in an interview setting.

Once the steps and skills have been identified, videotape the process with a familiar person presenting interview questions.

Considerations: Consider whether or not the individual is going to be interviewed by a single person or a group. (Sometimes individuals with autism have difficulty when auditory input is coming from more than one source. If it is going to be a group of interviewers more preparation may be needed.) Determine whether or not the individual is going to use an augmentative communication device and/or visual supports. If so, consider how to include this information in the video. After they have practiced with a familiar person, practicing with an unfamiliar person may be necessary. Consider varying the questions that are being asked to assist with generalization and also varying the order of the questions. Build in a relaxation routine prior to the interview (for some it may be important to videotape it).

EXAMPLES: Specific job skills

> "Only 6% of individuals with autism spectrum disorder have full-time employment. Only 12% of individuals with Asperger's or high functioning autism have full-time employment despite an average IQ. 22% have IQ's in the superior to very superior range. Adults say that finding a job would improve their lives more than anything else." (Barnard et al. 2001)

Goal: To increase job skills on a specific job site.

Implementation: Once a person has landed a job or is being considered for a job, videotape them or a co-worker performing the complete set of tasks that will be necessary for the specific job. Have the individual watch the video before going to work.

Considerations: In addition to teaching new job skills, video technology can be used to support an individual who has experienced some sort of breakdown on the job. New supports can be inserted into the job routine and videotaped.

A young adult with autism was temporarily suspended from his job of nine years because he threw a stapler at work. Through a series of written questions with multiple-choice answers, he was able to explain that the pictures in his head were "blaring out" and that throwing the stapler was a strategy he employed to get the pictures moving. When his team met with the job supervisor, it was learned that his long-held job had recently changed dramatically. He packaged items on an assembly line and the packaging changed. Pictures "blared out" for this young man each time he attempted to pick up packaging material that didn't "match" the picture of the (former) packaging material in his head. The team took photos of each step of his familiar routine with the new packaging and posted it for him at his job station. He reported that pictures no longer "blared out" at work. While this was a still photo array, the solution could have been done as a short video or the photos could have been downloaded onto a handheld electronic device for ease of viewing and discretion.

EXAMPLES: Loading a pop machine

> "Many children with autism are good at drawing, art and computer programming. These talent areas should be encouraged. I think there needs to be much more emphasis on developing the child's talents. Talents can be turned into skills that can be used for future employment." (Grandin 2002)

Goal: To increase employment skills by learning the job skill of loading a pop machine.

Implementation: Storyboard the steps involved. Most pop machines need a key to open the machine to begin loading. Acquisition of the key and using the key to open the machine are skills that may need to be pre-taught.

Considerations: Given the enormity of sensory experiences involved with loading a pop machine (e.g., temperature, sound, texture, lights), you may want to support the process with still pictures first.

Jay is a tenth-grade student with autism. He has successfully learned many job-related skills through the use of video modeling. When the task of loading the pop machines in his school was presented to him, Jay initially had difficulty with the task, as he was very sensitive to temperature change. His teacher videotaped the sequence and had Jay watch the routine every day prior to loading the machine. When the videotape reached the part where Jay would be putting his hand in the cold machine, his teacher had him touch a cold item. This process allowed Jay to internalize the changes in temperature and after a short period of time, he was independent at the task and now loads all of the machines weekly in his high school.

EXAMPLES: Urinal choice

> "Experience has shown that briefing ahead of time demystifies situations. Anticipating stimuli and talking about it ahead of time, while giving him strategies to work around possible problems, helps him cope with his surroundings." (Margaret Janger Flynn in Ariel and Naseef 2006)

Goal: To increase understanding of the "unwritten social rules and expectations of behavior that we all seem to know, but were never taught" (Bieber 1994). An example of an unwritten social rule and expectation can be determining urinal choice in a men's bathroom.

Implementation: Set up PowerPoint slides for review. Take pictures of each step: entering the bathroom; when and if to acknowledge others in the bathroom; choosing the appropriate urinal (i.e., space between individuals in bathroom); when using the urinal, where to look and not to look; conversational scripts in the bathroom; washing and drying hands; exiting the bathroom. Before using the bathroom, have the individual review pictures and practice scenarios.

Considerations: Additional stressors in a bathroom environment need consideration as they may impact the individual's access to information previously acquired: sensitivities to sound (e.g., automatic and manual flushing, noise of hand dryers, lights, echo of people's voices, etc.); location of bathroom (i.e., familiar setting vs. unfamiliar setting). When using a PowerPoint presentation to teach skill, consider adding text or audio cues for each step.

EXAMPLES: Using a cell phone

> "If there were only social people, we'd still be living in caves, talking." (Temple Grandin)

Goal: To maximize independence within the context of functional routines by learning to use a cell phone.

Implementation: Given that there are many different styles of cell phones, it will be important to teach skills with the specific brand and model of phone to be used. From the perspective of the person using the phone, videotape the sequences and the skills that are required: making a call; receiving a call; checking voicemail; looking up addresses and phone numbers; text messaging; leaving a message on another person's phone; using tools (e.g., calculator, calendar, camera); for cell phones that have Internet access (e.g., Blackberry, iPhone, Smartphone, etc.), access to email. Individual routines may need to be supported with visuals, including a task analysis. A visual of the calling plan with the best times to call, as well as a means of tracking used minutes, might be provided and included in the video of the skill sequence.

Considerations: The video should reference the specific brand and model of cell phone that the person owns, addressing the phone's features, the calling plan (number of minutes, calling, texting) and the service plan. In addition to learning to make/receive phone calls and texts, a person needs to be able to track minutes or call the service number regularly to check minutes left in a billing cycle, determine what time of day/night to use which functions, based on the service plan, and how to call for assistance if the phone malfunctions. These skills can all be made into videotaped skill sequences for the individual to learn, one at a time.

For people who do not speak, the texting function is a vital one for them. It is necessary to assess whether or not a person prefers to text with thumbs or with an individual index finger. It may be helpful to have a visual of the texting shortcuts and abbreviations until they are memorized by the person.

Life experiences

EXAMPLES: Decorating for holidays

> "While many happily anticipate the coming holiday season, families of people on the autism spectrum also understand the special challenges that may occur when schedules are disrupted and routines broken." (Autism Society of America 2010)

Goals: To assist individuals in processing and preparing for the changes that come with decorating for the holidays.

Implementation: Shoot a video of what your home will look like when it is decorated for a holiday celebration. (This is a video that is most easily shot after the celebration of the current holiday, for the next year.) Then, show the video to the individual during the weeks that precede your decorating, allowing them time to process the changes that are going to happen.

When Annalise, a young girl with autism, was at school one day during the holiday season, her mother decorated their house. When Annalise returned home from school that day, she became frightened. Repeatedly, she asked where her family had gone. Had they moved away? Her family was unable to comfort her for many days. The frequency of Annalise's tantrums increased and she also developed a new behavior: attempting to run away from home. The autism consultant working with the family theorized that Annalise no longer "recognized" her home due to the decorations. It was recommended that her mother take down all of the holiday decorations from the house. When her mother did so, the tantrums and running away behaviors ceased. A further recommendation was given to the family to slowly put up the decorations with Annalise present and videotape the transformation to better prepare her for the next year's holiday season. In this way, video can assist Annalise to integrate the visual changes that occur in her home during the holiday season. It may be important for Annalise's family to put decorations in the same location, or to videotape the changes of decoration placement in their home.

Considerations: It may be helpful to videotape from a number of different angles. Consider how the individual might be viewing the environment. If you do not have a video ready before the holiday, consider a low-tech option of using a picture of your home and then drawing directly onto the photo or onto a clear-plastic overlay to depict what your home will look like when it is decorated. If you have a lot of decorations, consider making the changes slowly to your home, changing only a few things at a time. For some individuals, it can be helpful if most of the decorations are placed in the same location of the house, classroom or work environment from year to year.

EXAMPLES: Going to a wedding

> "I rapidly am beginning to open my world to include other folks other than just my family and a few close friends or acquaintances." (Wally Wojtowicz, Jr. in Young 2010)

Goals: To assist individuals in processing and preparing for the (sometimes major) event of attending or being in a wedding.

Implementation: Watch videos with the individual that illustrate the possibilities of what might take place during the ceremony and after at the reception. For example, *Father of the Bride* (1959, 1991), *My Best Friend's Wedding*

(1997), *My Big Fat Greek Wedding* (2002). Film the wedding rehearsal, get permission to film others' weddings; film the venue where the event will be held. Use old home videos from family members or friends who are willing to share.

Considerations: If the individual is in the wedding and has to wear specific formal clothing, wearing the items ahead of time may be useful in identifying any unforeseen sensory sensitivities.

An event like a wedding has a lot of opportunities for insults to sensitive sensory systems. Depending on the size and type of wedding, the individual may be in a place they have never been before and there could be a lot of strangers around. There may be new or unusual food being served. If there is a dance as part of a reception, there will probably be loud music and flashing lights. When you shoot or view a video to prepare someone for an event like this, try to find out as much information about the specifics from the hosts as possible. Then, include this information in the video or choose clips that most closely match the event as described.

EXAMPLES: **Parades**

> "My senses are so hyper-aware, that the most ordinary sound or touch or movement causes a reaction of epidemic proportions." (Beth Adler in Ariel and Naseef 2006)

Goals: To assist individuals in processing and preparing for a special event like a parade.

Implementation: So many of our friends that have autism want to celebrate events with the rest of us, but the sights, sounds, smells and unexpected tactile input often make it very difficult for them. Unless you have access to filming a specific parade before it occurs, you may want to use YouTube videos to show a variety of video clips of parades.

The "YouTube method" is how we prepared a second-grade boy for the upcoming homecoming parade in his town. This was a child that had never sat through a parade before, but usually had difficulty in events like assemblies where there was excitement and noise. For a week before the big event, the child was given two or three videos to watch on YouTube that contained clips of parades that were similar in size and make-up to the parade he was going to be watching. At the event, he was able to sit through the entire parade without leaving the scene once.

Considerations: Make sure that you get shots of all of the things that could be included in the parade (bands, floats, vehicles, balloons, horses, etc.). Offer noise-reducing headphones or earplugs for the person with autism to assist with the noise level that often accompanies parades. Consider seating at a parade that will keep the person with autism out of the path of flying candy. Consider a seating or standing arrangement that will allow an "escape route" for the individual with autism, should they become overwhelmed and need to leave the setting.

EXAMPLES: Remodeling

> "It explains why, when there is a lot happening around me, I feel the whole world is imploding into my head." (Simon Brodie in Ariel and Naseef 2006)

Goals: To assist individuals in processing and preparing for the changes that come with making physical alterations in their living environment.

Implementation: There is software that allows you to preview the changes in your environment before you make them. One example of this technology is the "Personal Color Viewer" on the Benjamin Moore website. This website will allow you to upload a picture of what your current room or house looks like and then it will let you change the color, so you will be able to see what it will look like with a new color paint (www.benjaminmoore.com/personalcolorviewer).

Another variation of using software of this type is to simply take photographs of the current environment and then draw or color the changes you will make directly onto the picture. You may even want to videotape yourself making these changes on your model, to show the process.

Considerations: I remember a story that a grandmother of an autistic child told me. They were doing some remodeling in her house and stripped the carpeting off a flight of stairs, revealing a beautiful hardwood floor underneath. Immediately after this happened, her grandson lost the ability to go up and down the stairs at her house, even though he was able to navigate both carpeted and hardwood stairs at his own house. I wished that I could go back in time for this grandparent and do some of this visual foreshadowing with her grandson, to help prepare him for what to him was a drastic, dramatic change.

Consider how the individual themselves might be viewing the environment. If they are a child, you might want to get down to their eye-level to see what the current environment looks like and picture how things might look when they have changed. If the project is going to have phases, it may be important to illustrate the different phases in order.

EXAMPLES: Vacations

> "I felt safe in 'my world' and hated anything that tried to call me out of there..." (Williams 1994)

Goal: To assist individuals in processing and preparing for a special event like a vacation.

Implementation: Many of today's larger hotels and resorts have websites that allow you to access pictures and videos of the grounds. In the past, we have helped individuals prepare for vacations by developing PowerPoint presentations using these pictures interspersed with information about the hotel where they will be staying. Examine maps of the hotel or resort. Search for possible places to dine. Find out if the hotel or resort has a promotional DVD that they can send to you.

Considerations: If you are able to, find out which aspects of this area are the most important for the individual to know about.

EXAMPLES: Birth of a sibling

> "Whenever possible, we can help those with ASD by providing advanced notice about change, along with relevant information that can help them to understand the need for change, how to navigate the change, and what will stay the same in spite of the change." (Falvo 2009)

Goals: To assist individuals in processing the changes that will take place in their life due to the birth of a sibling.

Implementation: Watch videos with the individual about having a new sibling. Process the video with the individual. It may help the individual to have a visual way to process the things that will be the same and the things that will be different when the new sibling arrives, and to make a PowerPoint or photo visual of the differences. Possible activities that will support the upcoming transition are: going through baby pictures; visiting friends who have infants; packing a bag for the hospital; thinking of potential baby names; going to the doctor to hear the baby's heartbeat.

Considerations: Have the individual make a list of interview questions about siblings and make a video of himself conducting interviews of others who have siblings and how it impacted them. Then, watch the interviews and graph the answers to provide a prediction of how it might affect the individual. It would be particularly helpful to have the individual interview others with autism, or post interview questions in chat rooms and on websites (e.g., autismhub.org). Use videos of this type to assist with other new "additions" such as bringing home a new pet or changes such as a sibling going to college or a parent traveling for work.

CHAPTER SIX

Strengthening supports and teaching others

Video technology and individual supports

There are a variety of individual supports that a person with autism might find useful in navigating their world. Visual schedules, volume or emotional barometers, choice and menu boards and relationship wheels are just a few of the visual supports that have assisted individuals in regulating, understanding and interacting across environments. Video technology can offer guidance in using their individual supports with more consistency and independence.

Visual schedule

Many people with autism benefit from visual schedules that depict their day's activities in the order of occurrence. While some people fade to a written schedule or date book, it is important to honor the person's personal preference. This preference may be based on how the person processes incoming information. For some, pictures may be more effective than a written schedule, even if the person is able to read. Judy Endow describes her experience (personal communication, August 2009), which highlights this point: "When I am disregulated, verbal words are the first thing that loses meaning and written words are the next thing that loses meaning. This is why pictures might be important for individuals who read."

Relationship wheel

In order to answer a question about relationships that one person posed, a relationship wheel was created. This wheel is made up of circles of differing colors. Each circle represents a level of relationship: center circle represents "significant other/romantic partner"; first circle after the center circle represents "family and close friends"; second circle after the center circle represents "friends"; third circle after the center circle represents "acquaintances."

There are velcroed pieces of laminated paper on each circle, on which the actual names of different people in someone's life are written. This allows the

Relationship Wheel

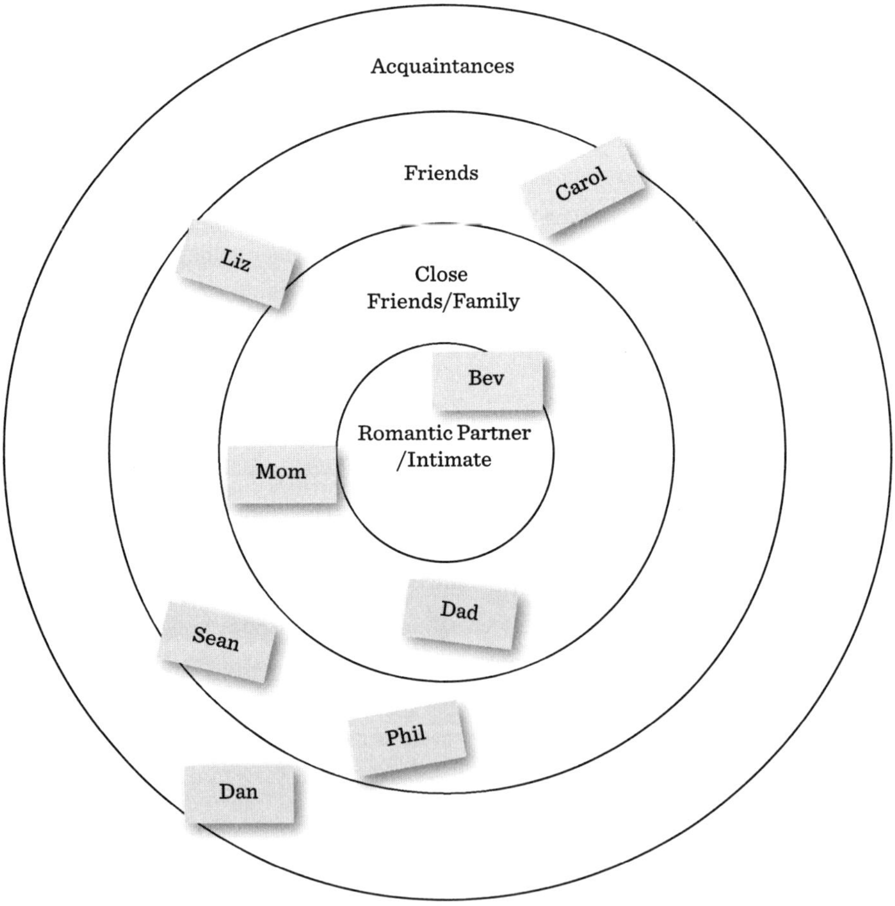

names to be moved from acquaintance to friend to close friend and so on, as relationships change. There is also a sheet that correlates with each level of the circle, which is labeled with the relationship type (i.e., significant other; family; close friends; friends; acquaintances). The person can use the sheet as a reminder of what kinds of interactions are matched with that relationship level. For instance, on the romantic level, one might write intercourse, long kisses, heavy petting, etc., while on the close family/friends level, one might write long hugs, kiss on the cheek, etc. This wheel can then be used to assist individuals in understanding what type of interactions are acceptable at each level of relationship. As relationships change, the person can move the names and then update the sheets that correlate to each relationship level.

Volume meter

Sometimes a person with autism may not be able to modulate his voice to match the situation. In such cases, the use of a volume meter might be used to provide a visual cue for each level of voice a person might need. For instance, in a school setting, a student might have a meter with pictures that signify a very quiet voice, such as in a test-taking situation; an indoor "classroom" voice; a lunchroom/hallway/gymnasium voice and an outside voice. (See diagram on page 66.)

Choice board

Being able to make choices can be supported by providing a person with a menu board of what their choices are in a given situation. For instance, before going to

When I feel angry, these are some things I can do:

- Squeeze my squish ball 
- Take a walk 
- Get a drink of water 
- Go swing 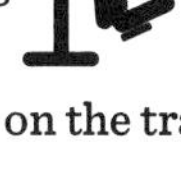
- Go jump on the trampoline 

recess, one might show a student a picture of all the options that are open to them, such as playground equipment, hula hoops, playground balls, tether ball, etc. Choice boards can be helpful for individuals in navigating the world and supporting their neurology in pulling up the pictures they need at the time they need them.

Teaching about autism

A person may want to explain to others how autism manifests in himself. A teacher may want to train staff to systematically teach an individual how to write her name. Parents may want staff to have a sense of their son/daughter's history. An adult may want to have a document of their employment skills, which can be shared with potential employers. All of these are ways that call out for the use of video technology to simplify and streamline the information being shared with others. It saves in meeting time, insures that everyone receives the same information, and provides the opportunity for an individual about whom the video/PowerPoint, etc. is being made to be included in the process.

Program consistency

One aspect of staff training in which video technology can be useful is obtaining program consistency. A visual recording can clearly depict types of cues and correction procedures that are used, how data is to be recorded, the most useful ways of supporting and redirecting an individual, and much other useful programming information.

Teaching methodology

When a particular type of teaching methodology is determined to be useful, video technology can insure it is used correctly and optimally for the individual. For instance, one team discovered that discrete trial format was effective for one of their students. There were eight people on the team who would be implementing DTF to teach academics, communication and social skills to this individual. In order to make sure that everyone knew how to use DTF in the same manner to insure consistency, they videotaped the lead teacher using DTF with the student. The team viewed the tape together and discussed it. Further, each team member was periodically videotaped using DTF with the student, which allowed the lead teacher to determine if any inadvertent mistakes were being made in implementation.

EXAMPLES: Demonstrating individual supports

> "Why can someone with Exposure Anxiety be expressively and naturally laughing out loud out in the back garden but somehow 'stuck,' compliant, or performing when in front of others? Why they can't get together to make breakfast once you are up, or run the bath, or get dressed, but seem to do a whole range of these things, which might prove they were capable of these? Why might someone with Exposure Anxiety be able to imitate communication with their own reflection and yet unable to respond as themselves when shown affection? Or be able to initiate an activity, but when you try to initiate exactly the same activity with them, appear uninterested, distracted or disowning? Why, although they have the ability, do they appear to freeze and become incapable in front of others or when asked to perform a task on command?" (Williams 2003)

Goal: To introduce a new individual support or to strengthen the consistency of use of an existing individual support.

Implementation: Videotape, make a PowerPoint, or use some other kind of video technology to record a student using their individual support or someone else demonstrating the use of an individual support.

A student with autism had been using a visual schedule for a couple of years. While this seemed helpful to him, his team determined that he needed more information for each activity picture on his schedule. They wanted to teach him how a "schedule within a schedule" worked. A "schedule within a schedule" has an activity picture and then a strip listing the subparts of the activity. For instance, there may be a picture of circle time for a younger student and the schedule within a schedule strip might have calendar, attendance song, colors, and Halloween countdown, on it, as each of these are portions of the circle time. To teach the student how this worked, the teacher downloaded the visual schedule to her computer and projected it onto a Smart Board. As she presented each subpart, she removed the picture from the strip and put it in a "done" file on the Smart Board, while the student was assisted to do the same with his personal Velcro version of the schedule in front of him. This taught him how to use it without any distraction to the other students.

Considerations: Videotape all the different uses of the individual support to assist the person in generalizing to all needed situations. One might consider having a peer model use of the support in the video. It is generally helpful for the person to watch the video immediately before the time they will need to access that skill.

EXAMPLES: **Peer sensitivity**

> "Regardless of the age and level of challenge experienced by an individual with autism or the structure of service delivery, there will undoubtedly be a need to teach the people surrounding that person about who he or she is. These people can use the teachings to be appropriately responsive to the educational, emotional, social, communication, and spiritual needs presented by someone with autism." (McGinnity and Negri 2005)

Goal: To teach peers of autistic individuals.

Implementation: Video technology is an effective means for people to describe their autism to peers and how it affects their relationships and learning. Ben, a fourth-grade student with autism felt that his classmates needed to know more about him, what he loves and how he outsmarts his autism. Along with his teacher, Ben made a PowerPoint presentation, accompanied by several videos, and presented it to his entire class.

Considerations: When conducting any kind of sensitivity training, it is important to include the family if the individual is a minor. Families can often provide important aspects of the person that are useful to share with others. Also, some families have a preference about information they do not want shared, and it is important to consider this before making a video.

Some people wish to be the director, writer and primary cast of their video. Others want some creative control, but do not wish to be directly involved in making or appearing in their video/PowerPoint. Always try to honor the person's wishes in determining their level of participation. When making a video or PowerPoint for peer sensitivity, remember to consider the audience. For younger viewers, the presentation should be brief and concise. In fact, for younger audiences, it may be helpful to use several short clips that can be viewed over time. Also, for younger children, it is often helpful to view a presentation repeated times, to increase their learning and attention to it.

For school-aged individuals, it is helpful to check in with the primary teacher(s) to determine if the peer sensitivity video/PowerPoint presentation can be imbedded in the curriculum in some way. For instance, language arts teachers have used peer sensitivity presentations as the impetus for writing exercises;

civics teachers have used them as a spark to ignite discussions on personal rights/freedoms; and math teachers have used peer sensitivity presentations to illustrate percentages and probabilities.

EXAMPLES: Showcasing employment skills

"It is by developing our talents that we can step more easily into the work world and find jobs that are a good fit for us." (Grandin and Duffy 2004)

Goal: To increase employment for individuals with autism.

Implementation: People with autism often have expansive employment skills but cannot show them in an interview format. There may be questions from a potential employer based on perceived competence. By videotaping individuals completing tasks and assignments and then showing the video at job interviews, employers have a more accurate perspective about the potential employee.

Jonathan is a tenth-grade student who is nonverbal and has autism. When his teacher began seeking out potential job opportunities in the community, employers were skeptical about what Jonathan would be able to do, how they would communicate with him and the level of supervision he would need. When his teacher showed various videos of him completing a series of different jobs, employers were suddenly open to hiring Jonathan. Two of his current employers have offered continued work once he has graduated.

Considerations: When putting together video clips for potential employers, include a variety of different types of skills in a variety of settings to demonstrate a person's flexibility and full breadth of abilities. If any type of augmentation or accommodation is necessary for the person's success, reflect its use in the video.

EXAMPLES: Adult training video

"It is so hard to meet new people and to say goodbye. I miss so many people from the past. I never see them, it is so lonely. I want to see them so bad. Why don't they want to see me? I am happy to share. I love others." (Roy Bedward)

Goal: The goal of having adults with ASD make a training video for their staff and significant people in their lives is threefold: self-advocacy, sensitivity training and staff skill training. Having the person with ASD involved in the development, script and production of the video insures that the video reflects what is important to this person and the kinds of supports that are most useful, as well as what is not useful. Lisa, a young adult with autism who types to talk opened her staff training video by typing that she is not stupid and implored that staff not talk down to her or treat her like a baby.

The video may include collaborative supports at home, in the community and in work sites. Some people prefer to write a script and narrate their own video, while others may request information from another. David, 25, requested that a support person who had been in his life co-narrate his video with him. Together, they wrote a script, with David determining which sections he wanted to speak/read and which ones he wanted his support person to speak/read.

Implementation: Determine the primary audience for the video (in-home staff, vocational staff, family, friends, etc.) and what the person wants this audience to know about them. Collaborate with the person about what portion they want to do and whether or not they want to have a co-narrator or "guest speaker." One young adult requested that her friend (who happened to be an autism consultant) be part of her video as a guest speaker explaining about movement disorders and how they affected her day-to-day access to her skills. Film a video of the person(s) doing the narration. It may be useful to include a video of the individual at various community sites, work sites and with family/friends, so the staff has a sense of a rounded and complete life.

Considerations: Think through what information will be shared with the viewers, such as: description of autism neurology; level of intelligence; family history; individual dreams. It may be helpful to depict what types of supports are useful (e.g., less or more talking; use of visual schedule; starting over when their body gets stuck), as well as what kinds of supports are not useful (verbally repeating something over and over or talking loudly; unexpected or unwanted physical assistance). Share what is important to the individual in relationships (e.g., trust; knowing when a person's body and movement doesn't always cooperate; a shared vision of independence).

With younger individuals or people who are either unable or don't prefer to participate in the narration, it can be helpful to have another person do the narrating. Collaborate with the individual on the script, as much as possible. At the very least, they should read or be read the script for final approval. Some individuals have conducted interviews of different significant people in their lives as part of their staff training videos (family, friends, classmates, co-workers).

EXAMPLES: Data taking and observational accuracy skills

> "Applied behavior analysis (ABA) is the science of human behavior. ABA focuses on the reliable measurement and objective evaluation of observable behavior." (MADSEC 2000)

Goals: To assist team members in developing accurate measures of behavioral observation and insure consistency between members in data tracking.

Implementation: Videotape the individual displaying the targeted behavior. Have team members watch the video. While members are watching the video, have them track the specified behaviors using a behavior tracking system. As a team, have members share their data. Evaluate the data. Make changes to definition of the target behavior and behavior intervention plans as needed to insure consistency in tracking the behavior. To expedite this process, team members do not have to view the video as a group. Have members watch the same video at different times, do their tracking, and then come together to share their data. Teams should always have the tape available for viewing when they are evaluating the data. Reviewing the tape will help identify subtle behavioral cues or changes in environment.

Considerations: Consider using the videotape method as a means of training new team members on taking data. The data tracking does not necessarily have to be formalized. Using the video, team members could analyze the behaviors and share objective feedback.

EXAMPLES: Skill sampling portfolio

> "Current assessment instruments may be inadequate to capture change that is important to patients and families, and thus recent reports document discordant findings." (King 2003)

Goal: To assist individuals in tracking progress and changes over time.

Implementation: Videotape the individual in setting. Wait a predetermined amount of time. Take another video. To achieve the most reliability in videotaping, this predetermined amount of time should be as consistent as possible. The amount of time between the videos will depend upon what you are tracking and the rate of changes that the individual is making. Be sure to take enough footage so that a true sample of the individual or designated skill is obtained. Videotape across environments, with other individuals involved, different days, different times of day, etc.

Considerations: Videotape current levels of functioning, i.e., a sampling of work for a Present Level of Performance (see glossary). When using video sampling as a means to illustrate Present Level of Performance on an IEP, be sure to attach a DVD to the document or include a note in the IEP that the video is part of the document. Consider using video technology to track performance on a specific skill, such as learning to read. Before using video as an official means of measuring progress, be sure to obtain district/administrative approval.

CHAPTER SEVEN

Just do it

Overcoming fear

Perhaps the biggest obstacle to using video technology is our own fear. Technology changes at breathtaking speed and it often feels like there is more to learn than there is time to learn it. Part of overcoming fear is knowing where to go for help. There are many avenues: other colleagues who have a knack for and interest in technology; the Web person or technology person at your school or place of employment; websites that explain and offer technical support. For those of us lucky enough to be parenting an adolescent with a passion for technology, they become our built-in support. Help is out there. Our point is to "just do it." Video technology can make a strikingly positive difference in the lives of many autistic people.

To leave the reader with some inspiration, we are providing stories from teachers and caregivers who, like ourselves, overcame their obstacle of fear to use video technology with someone in their life who has autism. Below are their stories. Read and be inspired!

STORIES: Katherine Rybak, Sun Prairie Wisconsin Public Schools

I have used video modeling for more than one student. With one boy who has autism, we used a handheld Flip video camera to record him acting out social stories. He watches these videos daily and has learned to manage stressful situations by mimicking the behaviors he sees on the video. He has an intrinsic interest in drama and acting, so the videos are great for motivating him to use his acting skills for emotional regulation.

I also work with a middle-school boy with significant autism who struggles to learn basic daily living skills and to control his behaviors. For him, we have utilized two separate video cameras. One camera is used for recording and viewing instructional social videos and living samples of excellent behaviors. The other camera contains reward videos of buses, trains, and favorite TV clips. This highly mobile reward camera is given to the student as soon as he demonstrates a behavior or meets criteria for a reward. We have used this system to teach skills such as ordering independently at a restaurant, cleaning his room, and following a bedtime routine without verbal cues. He is willing to work extra hard knowing he will have access to his favorite videos immediately after completing a task, no matter where we are. The cameras are simple to use. It is easy to add new skills and new rewards. The system is easily implemented in all environments with all caregivers.

A young girl uses her video camera to capture moments in her life, such as visiting relatives, holiday celebrations, and playing with friends. We use these videos as language stimulation scenes, helping her describe real-life events by watching them happen over and over again, and eliminating the chore of recalling details from memory. Both her verbal expression and written expression benefit from this method. Additionally, she is able to easily share important social information with her family and friends by sharing her videos and thereby increasing her social connections.

STORIES: **Kathy Kaebisch, Speech/Language Pathologist, Germantown Wisconsin School District**

As a speech and language pathologist employed in a public school setting, working on social skills is a high priority with my students who are on the autism spectrum. Several years ago, three of these students on my caseload desperately needed a new approach to work on their social skills. Video modeling was one suggestion that I received. I had my doubts about the effectiveness of this new technique. But as I began using video modeling, the results were immediate and positive.

In their eyes, my three students became "movie stars" and their therapy sessions became dress rehearsals and final takes. Seeing themselves performing social activities on a TV set or projected on a movie screen was extremely motivating. This was such a popular activity that the entire school became aware of it and we began to incorporate classroom peers into the video modeling sessions with excellent results. However, the best part of all was and still is the unbelievable carryover of the social skills that we modeled into my students' academic, social, home and community lives. I received overwhelmingly positive feedback from many teachers, parents, coaches, aides and peers as to the noticeable improvements that my "movie stars" were displaying.

STORIES: **Lisa Hoeme, MS, CRC, autism consultant**

As an autism consultant I'm always looking for new and effective strategies to help teach and support individuals with autism. When I first heard about video modeling, I thought it sounded like a good match for the learning style of many people that I support. In the beginning I was a little intimidated by the technology and worried that it would be extremely time consuming. After trying it a few times, I discovered that my experience was the complete opposite. It was actually quick and easy. Most importantly, I found that not only is it an effective teaching tool, but also most individuals with autism have fun and enjoy making the videos as well.

One of my favorite stories is about David, a six-year-old boy on the autism spectrum. I had begun to work closely with his family on helping him become more independent with some of his daily living routines. His mother mentioned that one of her biggest concerns was that David doesn't put his seatbelt on. And if he does it is often not long before she looks back and he has taken it off. We decided to try using video modeling to teach him to put his seatbelt on and to keep it on until they arrive at their destination. To prepare we wrote a simple list of the steps involved. David was very excited the first time I brought the camera to his house. With his brother co-starring, we videotaped the two boys getting into their car, putting their seatbelts on, wearing their seatbelts while riding and taking them off once they arrived at the destination.

David wanted to watch the video several times immediately after we recorded it and seemed very excited to see himself on film. Using simple video editing software that came standard on my computer, I made a few quick edits to take out any extraneous cues or distractions and added a few title slides that outlined the steps of the routine. David loved to watch the video and after the first day of watching it he independently put on and wore his seatbelt to the store. They continued to have the same success in traveling to other places and no longer had to worry that he would take his seatbelt off in the car. We've now used video modeling both to help David learn new things and to develop independence. It has become a very effective teaching tool. David continues to have fun making videos and has now even asked to have videos made when something new is coming up or when he is having a hard time understanding a routine or social situation.

STORIES: **Your story here**

Can you imagine ways in which you, dear reader, might use video technology to support your students or friends with autism? We hope our book has inspired you to try something new, something different, or to continue something that is already working for the autistic people in your lives ...

SUPPLEMENTAL DVD CONTENTS

Aaron's PowerPoint. Created by sixth-grader Aaron Emory in collaboration with his speech and language therapist as part of his transition into middle school. He presented the PowerPoint at his annual Individual Education Plan (IEP) team meeting at the end of his sixth-grade year to his entire IEP team and all of his upcoming seventh-grade teachers. Afterwards Aaron took questions from his upcoming teachers. This was the first IEP meeting that Aaron had attended. Song: "(A) Wish for You" by August McWake and Lucas Bielejewski. (Purposes: Supporting and strengthening relationships; Supporting transition)

Staff training video. Video compiled by an autism consultant for the purpose of staff development. The team noticed that there was ongoing turnover among the staff supporting the individual and that it was becoming increasingly difficult to train everyone in an efficient manner. Videotaping the consultant was a cost-effective way to ensure that all staff members were receiving the same information in a timely manner. (Purpose: Staff training.)

Noah's PowerPoint. PowerPoint presentation developed for a first-grade class. It provided autism sensitivity and education for Noah's classmates (some of whom knew him from kindergarten and some of whom he had never had class with before). The presentation laid the groundwork for children in the class to ask questions about Noah or about autism. It gave them a forum to talk about how not everyone in their class learns in the same way. The PowerPoint also gave the children tools to use in their interactions with Noah. His parents reported that they saw a difference in the interactions of the children the same day the presentation was given. (Purpose: Sensitivity.)

John's PowerPoint. PowerPoint created by teachers of a high school student with Asperger's syndrome and the student, to assist his current staff in better understanding him and his needs. The team also used this PowerPoint to support John with transitioning to new teachers the following year, allowing them to save time in meetings regarding his specific strengths and needs. John participated in many aspects of creating the PowerPoint, especially the sheet of what is happening for him when he puts his head down on his desk. As a result of doing this project with him, staff members reported learning some new things about how he experiences the world. (Purposes: Transition; Staff training.)

Nichela's PowerPoint. Single PowerPoint slide idea developed by a team in Elkhorn, Wisconsin, to assist a student in transitioning from fourth to fifth grade. Each of the students in fourth grade made a PowerPoint slide that included their name, photo, and some information about their interests. Once the class lists were posted in August, his mom pulled together the slides of his upcoming classmates. He spent the last weeks of August reviewing the slides of the students with whom he would be sharing a classroom, thus enhancing his social comfort and knowledge of classmates ahead of time. (Purpose: Transition.)

Northside Elementary video. Video created by three staff members at Northside Elementary School in Middleton, Wisconsin. Connie Sue Prochnow (SLP), Angela Norman (SLP) and Jennifer Latek (OT) put the video together as a way of foreshadowing a new school environment to incoming students with autism or other special needs. The video has been popular with students, parents, and staff at the school and has been adapted and updated with each new school year. (Purpose: Transition.)

Washing hands PowerPoint. Created by a special education teacher whose student needed those who supported him to verbally cue him to complete the steps in washing his hands. The student would wait by the sink for the support staff to give him a cue for each individual step although he could complete the physical movements of the task. Audio prompts were added to each step. The PowerPoint was shown to the student during the task and in book format outside of the task. The teacher faded both the sound and the PowerPoint as the student began initiating the steps of the task. The end result was complete independence for the student. (Purpose: Self-care/ADLs.)

Tying shoes video. Developed to assist a student in learning to tie her shoes. The video was shot from the perspective of the person tying their shoe and was presented to the student in her occupational therapy session prior to each teaching trial. The student requested the video in each session and watched attentively two or three times prior to attempting the task. She became successful in tying her shoes after approximately a month of viewing the video. (Purpose: Self-care/ADLs.)

Seatbelt video. Developed for an individual who was resisting the process of getting in the car, buckling his seatbelt and keeping the seatbelt on during the car ride. The video was shot of a peer, similar in size and age. It was viewed prior to leaving the house each time the individual was to get into the car to go somewhere. The video was reinforced at school as well. It was presented over a period of two weeks before the routine was independent for the individual. (Purpose: Self-care/ADLs.)

Microwave video. Developed "on the spot" as a result of a student who was significantly disregulated by the noise of the microwave, which was utilized by adults in the classroom in which he received instruction. Each time an adult entered the room with a cup/plate and maneuvered toward the microwave, the student would place his hands over his ears and make a loud noise. After removing the student from the room, staff videotaped the entire sequence of the microwave being used to heat up a cup of coffee. When the student was back in the room, the staff showed him the video of the sequence. This first viewing showed slight agitation and covering of the ears, the second hailed a significantly less agitated response and the third viewing produced no response from the student. This response generalized to the natural environment, no longer producing disregulation for the student. (Purpose: Desensitization.)

Riley's PowerPoint. PowerPoint presentation with imbedded video developed to help Noah, a child with autism who was sensitive about haircuts. The video was filmed with a favorite peer of Noah's. It was shot to replicate the same situations Noah would encounter (having his hair cut at home by a parent). Noah's parents showed him the video a number of times before attempting the procedure. Viewings were paired with some systematic desensitization in which Noah was rewarded for letting a parent cut gradually more pieces of his hair at a time. Now, Noah asks for haircuts and does not have any trouble sitting calmly during the process. (Purpose: Desensitization.)

Jack Othello's PowerPoint. PowerPoint social story created by a student, Jack, together with his autism consultant, Nan Negri. This PowerPoint was used to help Jack identify which behaviors were troublesome to him when responding to "hard energy" words from others and to provide him with alternative choices of what he could do instead. The first few PowerPoint slides describe the difference between what Jack and Nan labeled "hard energy" words and "soft energy" words. Scenes 1-4 depict what currently happened for Jack when he was "hit" with hard energy words* such as getting stuck or frozen, running away, hitting himself in the head and a behavioral explosion. Scenes 5-7 provide a menu of alternative positive choices for Jack to use when "hard energy" words are directed at him by others. The final alternative choice for Jack is to use square breathing: the student is coached to breathe in while an animated arrow travels up the left side of a square (or, if one doesn't have this on an animated PowerPoint slide, a finger could trace the arrow going up while the student is coached to breathe in). Next the student is coached to hold their breath in while the arrow moves along the top of the square, breathe out slowly while the arrow travels down the right side of the square and hold breath out again while the arrow travels along the bottom of the square. Square breathing can assist students in becoming calmer; when their breathing slows down, they often breathe more deeply into their bellies. This was the case for Jack. (Purposes: Sensory regulation; Behavioral support.)

*For many individuals with autism, visually depicting the troublesome behavior would make it difficult for them to inhibit that behavior. This was not the case for Jack. It's important to know the individual when determining whether or not to depict the behavior that is targeted for change.

GLOSSARY

Adaptive Living Skills. Skills needed to function in daily life, sometimes referred to as ADLs (activities of daily living). They can include grooming, housekeeping, recreation/leisure and community functioning.

Affirmation video. Video in which the viewer is shown positive images about themselves or experiences that they enjoy.

Applied Behavior Analysis (ABA). Teaching and shaping behavior through the use of carefully observed data coupled with positive reinforcement and prompting.

Augmentative Communication Device. A device for supporting and enhancing communication, usually used for people who do not have speech or cannot access their speech abilities consistently. Some devices have keyboards, others have pictures or words. May or may not have electronic or taped voice output.

Backwards chaining. Chaining procedure that breaks down the steps of a task and teaches them in reverse order.

Chaining. An instructional procedure based on applied behavior analysis in which a long sequence of behavior is broken down into smaller steps. Then, each step is reinforced as the individual is able to perform them successfully.

Comic Strip Conversations. Strategy developed by Carol Gray in her book of the same name (1994). Simple comic book drawings and balloon dialogue are used to map out the interpersonal give-and-take of a conversation.

Conversation bubble. Used in *Comic Strip Conversations.* A rounded outline coming out of the mouth of a drawn or sketched character, which represents the spoken word.

Desensitization. Behavioral therapy used to help people with autism and Asperger's syndrome overcome phobias and anxiety disorders. It can involve the use of relaxation techniques and graduated exposure therapy.

Discrete trial format. Teaching method that involves task analysis (i.e., breaking skills down into smaller components) and teaching those smaller components individually.

Discriminative stimulus (SD). Event or cue that provides information about what to do.

Echolalia. Repeating words or phrases that are said by another. While part of normal language acquisition in typical development, it is a lingering characteristic of the speech style of some people with autism.

Exposure anxiety. A process of self-protection, first described by Donna Williams in her book *Exposure Anxiety: The Invisible Cage* (2003). In the process, individuals engage in compulsive avoidance in order to avoid specific painful stimuli.

Extinction. Weakening a reinforced behavior through the graduated removal of reinforcement triggers.

Fading. Gradually removing a prompt so that a response becomes independent.

Feed forward. Type of video self-modeling in which individuals are shown video of themselves displaying a skill that they are not yet able to perform with independence.

Flip video. Easy to use compact digital video camcorder first introduced in 2006. While still in use and popular, the device was discontinued in 2011.

Forward chaining. Chaining procedure that begins with teaching the first step of the task and then progressing to each subsequent step.

Generalization. Demonstration of a behavior or skill across a number of environments and social settings.

Hidden curriculum. Rules governing social interactions that are universally understood without being directly taught.

Individual Education Plan (IEP). Public school special education document that describes goals, objectives and special support for a specific student; developed by the IEP team.

Instructional cue. Direction or instruction given to an individual that communicates what they need to do. A term used in Applied Behavior Analysis.

In-vivo (live) modeling. Type of modeling where a student observes other people model target behaviors with the goal of teaching the student how to perform the targeted skill.

iPad. Portable media player from Apple Computer with a 9.7-inch touch screen. It can play digital audio or video recordings, as well as a wide variety of other applications.

iPod Touch. Portable media player from Apple Computer. Approximately the size of a deck of playing cards, it can play digital audio or video recordings, as well as a wide variety of other applications.

Mean Length Utterance (MLU). The average length of an individual's spoken phrases of morphemes (the basic element of language). Higher MLUs indicate a higher level of language proficiency.

MP3 player. Generic name for any portable electronic device used for storing, organizing, and playing digital audio or video files. Examples include Apple iPod, Microsoft Zune, Sony Walkman, and SanDisk Sansa.

Natural environment. Teaching a skill in the "real world" (i.e., the environment where the skill will be applied). A term used in Applied Behavior Analysis.

Positive self-review. Type of video self-modeling in which an individual is shown video of themselves displaying a skill that they can perform, but do not have access to performing all the time. Viewed to help assist in generalization of a skill and to increase fluency and proficiency.

PowerPoint. Microsoft program used to develop presentations and organize information by creating a series of slides, which may contain text, pictures, audio or video clips.

Preparation video. Video used to help an individual get ready for an upcoming event or transition.

Prerequisite skills. Skills, concepts or ideas that an individual needs to understand prior to moving on to a subsequent skill.

Present Level of Performance (PLP). Section of IEP report that describes how a student is currently doing.

Proprioception. Internal bodily sense that relates where parts of the body are in relation to each other. Receptors located in joints and muscles. Together with the vestibular system, provides information as to whether the body is in movement and where it is located in relation to other aspects of the environment.

Reinforcement. Anything that strengthens or increases the probability of a response.

Self-advocacy video. Video that a person on the spectrum either creates themselves or asks others to create for them as a means of sharing information about themselves or their challenges.

Sensitivity video. Video used as a means to help others understand what it might be like to experience autism.

Sensory system. Part of the brain/nervous system that takes in information from the environment and processes it to regulate and determine response categories. Includes sight, hearing, somatic sensation (touch), taste and olfaction (smell). Also the vestibular and proprioceptive systems.

Shaping. Teaching new behavior gradually through progressive reinforcement.

Skill-teaching video. Video designed to teach new skills through informational instructions.

Skype. Computer program for phone calls and video conferencing over the Internet.

SMART Board. Interactive whiteboard developed by SMART Technologies. Allows for touch control of computer applications on a large-scale dry erase board.

Social networking websites. Internet sites such as Facebook, MySpace, and Twitter for individuals to focus on building social contacts. Often provide services to their users such as social interest groups, games, e-mail, and instant messaging.

Social script. Scenario for social interaction. Provides information on what to say and how to identify when to apply the script. (See appendix.)

Social story. Support strategy devised by Carol Gray (2000, 2010). Uses narrative storytelling to help visualize social situations, skills or concepts.

Staff-training video. Video used by support staff members for learning sensitivity skills and strategies for assisting their clients on the spectrum.

Storyboard. Preliminary series of pictures or sketches that sequence and outline the shots that will comprise a video. (See appendix.)

Task analysis. Breaking down a task into smaller step-by-step components.

Vestibular system. Internal bodily sense that provides information about where our bodies are in relation to the environment. Contributes to our balance and our sense of spatial orientation. Receptors located in the inner ear.

Video Modeling. Modeling a behavior or action on video with the intention of teaching a novel skill.

Video Self-Modeling. Viewing oneself on video performing a behavior or action, with the intention of learning a novel skill.

Video technology. Electronic tools that contain pictures that move or change. This includes, but is not limited to: analog or digital video tape from cameras; purchased videos or DVDs made for teaching specific skills; other video media like TV shows or movies, websites, computer programs, PowerPoint presentations; MP3 players, and other similar portable electronic devices; Skype, Smart Boards, and social networking programs.

REFERENCES

Alger, I. 1969. Therapeutic use of videotape playback. *Journal of Nervous and Mental Disease* 148: 430-436.

Ariel, C., and R. Naseef, eds. 2006. *Voices from the Spectrum: parents, grandparents, siblings, people with autism, and professionals share their wisdom.* London: Jessica Kingsley Publishers.

Attwood, T. 1998. *Asperger's Syndrome: A Guide for Parents and Professionals.* Philadelphia: Jessica Kingsley Publishers.

Attwood, T. 2000. Should children with an autistic spectrum disorder be exempted from doing homework? http://home.comcast.net/~jorghahaq/A3.htm.

Attwood, T. 2007. *The Complete Guide to Asperger's Syndrome.* London: Jessica Kingsley Publishers.

Attwood, T. 2009. Quotations. Web: tonyattwood.com

Autism is a World. Dir. Gerardine Wurzburg. CNN Productions, 2004. DVD.

Autism Society of America. 2010. Twelve tips for helping people with autism and their families have a happy holiday. http://www.autism-society.org/site/PageServer?pagename=holiday_tips

Bandura, A. 1969. *Principles of Behavior Modification.* New York: Holt, Reinhart and Winston.

Bandura, A. 1997. *Self-Efficacy: The Exercise of Control.* New York: Worth.

Baron, M. G., J. Groden, G. Groden, and L. P. Lipsitt. 2006. *Stress and Coping in Autism.* Oxford: Oxford University Press.

Barron, J., and S. Barron. 1992. *There's a Boy in Here.* New York: Simon and Schuster.

Bellini, S., J. Akullian, and A. Hopf. 2007. Increasing social engagement in young children with autism spectrum disorders using video self-modeling. School Psychology Review 36: 80-90.

Bettelheim, B. 1967. *The Empty Fortress: Infantile Autism and the Birth of the Self.* New York: The Free Press.

Betts, T. 1983. Developing a videotape library. In *Using Video: Psychological and social applications,* eds. P. Dowrick and S. Biggs, 61-71. New York: Wiley.

Biklen, D., ed. 2005. *Autism and the Myth of the Person Alone.* New York: NYU Press.

Browning, P., and W. White. 1986. Teaching life enhancement skills with interactivevideo-based curricula. *Education and Training of Mentally Retarded* 21: 236-244.

Buggey, T. 2008. Video self-modeling applications for young children with ASD. Presented at the Autism Society of America Conference, Orlando, FL.

Buggey, T. 2009. *Seeing Is Believing: Video Self-Modeling for People with Autism and Other Developmental Disabilities.* Bethesda: Woodbine House.

Buggey, T., K. Toombs, P. Gardener, and M. Cervetti. 1999. Training responding behaviors in students with autism: Using videotaped self-modeling. *Journal of Positive Behavior Interventions* 1: 205-214.

Burke, J. 2007. The Ideal School: How one small symbol of punctuation can change lives. Council of Parent, Attorneys and Advocates Conference. http://www.allstartapes.com/conferences/conference_1106.shtml.

Butch, G. 2010. Tips to improve haircuts for children with autism. http://ezinearticles.com/?Tips-to-Improve-Hair-Cuts-For-Children-With-Autism&id=1788427.

Carr, E., and M. Darcy. 1990. Setting generality for peer modeling in children with autism. *Journal of Autism and Developmental Disorders* 20: 45-49.

Cesaroni, L., and M. Garber. 1991. Exploring the experience of autism through first hand account. *Journal of Autism and Developmental Disorders* 21 (3): 303-313.

Charlop, M., and J. Milstein. 1989. Teaching autistic children conversational speech using video modeling. *Journal of Applied Behavior Analysis* 22 (3): 275-285.

Charlop, M., and M. Walsh. 1986. Increasing autistic children's spontaneous verbalizations of affection: An assessment of time delay and peer modeling procedures. *Journal of Applied Behavior Analysis* 35 (3): 213-231.

Charlop-Christy, M., and S. Daneshvar. 2003. Using video modeling to teach perspective taking to children with autism. *Journal of Positive Behavior interventions* 5: 12-21.

Charlop-Christy, M., L. Le, and K. Freeman. 2000. A comparison of video modeling with in vivo modeling for teaching children with autism. *Journal of Autism and Developmental Disorders* 30: 537-552.

Cohen, S. 2006. T*argeting Autism: what we know, don't know, and can do to help young children with autism spectrum disorders.* Berkeley: University of California Press.

D'Ateno, P., K. Mangiapanello, and B. Taylor. 2003. Using video modeling to teach complex play sequences to a preschooler with autism. *Journal of Positive Behavior Interventions* 5: 5-11.

Davis, K., and M. Dubie. 2004. Sensory integration: tips to consider. *The Reporter* 9 (3): 3-8. http://www.isdd.indiana.edu/irca/sensory/sensoryintegrate.html.

Debbaudt, D. 2001. Autism and airport travel safety tips. SATH. http://www.sath.org/index.php?sec=768&id=2371.

Donnellan, A., D. Hill, and M. Leary. 2010. Rethinking autism: Implications of sensory movement differences. *Disabilities Studies Quarterly* 30 (1).

Donnellan, A., M. Leary, and J. Robledo. 2006. I can't get started: Stress and the role of movement differences for individuals with the autism label. In *Stress and Coping in Autism*, eds. G. Baron, J. Groden, G. Groden and L. Lipsitt, 205-245. Oxford: Oxford University Press.

Donnellan, A. M., and M. R. Leary. 1995. Movement Differences and Diversity in Autism/Mental Retardation. Madison: DRI Press.

Donnellan, A. M., G. W. LaVigna, N. Negri-Shoultz, and L. L. Fassbender. 1986. *Progress without Punishment.* New York: Teachers College Press.

Dowrick, P., and S. Biggs, eds. 1983. *Using Video.* New York: Wiley.

Dowrick, P. 1983. Self-modeling. In *Using Video,* eds. P. Dowrick and S. Biggs, 61-71. New York: Wiley.

Dowrick, P., and T. Buggey. 2000. Creating futures through video self-modeling behavioral interventions: Social and academic development in challenging behaviors and autism. *Journal of Intellectual Disability Research* 44: 310.

Dubin, N. 2007. *Asperger Syndrome and Bullying: Strategies and Solutions.* Philadelphia: Jessica Kingsley Publishers.

Dunn Buron, K., and M. Curtis. 2003. *The Incredible 5- Point Scale.* Shawnee Mission, KS: Autism Asperger Publishing Company.

Dunn Buron, K. 2007. *A "5" Could Make Me Lose Control! An activity based method for evaluating and supporting highly anxious students.* Shawnee Mission, KS: Autism Asperger Publishing Co.

Endow, J. 2006. *Making Lemonade: Hints for Autism's Helpers.* Cambridge, WI: CBR Press.

Endow, J. 2009. How to float autism's boat. Presented as part of Wisconsin Department of Public Instruction Statewide Autism Training.

Endow, J. 2009. *Paper Words: Discovering and living with my autism.* Shawnee Mission, KS: Autism Asperger Publishing Company.

Falvey, M.A., M. Forest, J. Pearpoint, and R. L. Rosenberg. 1992. *All My Life's a Circle: Using the tools:* Circles, MAPS and PATHS. Toronto: Inclusion Press.

Falvey, M. A. 1989. *Community-Based Curriculum: Instructional strategies for students with severe handicaps.* Baltimore: Paul H. Brookes.

Falvo, Laurel. 2009. Autism and change. *Gray Center SUN News,* March 16. http://graycenter.wordpress.com/2009/03/16/the-autistic-brain-responds-to-change/.

Fuller, F., and B. Manning. 1973. Self-confrontation reviewed: a conceptualization for video playback in teacher education. *Review of Educational Research* 43: 469-528.

Gagnon, E. 2001. *Power Cards: Using special interests to motivate children and youth with asperger syndrome and autism.* Shawnee Mission, KS: Autism Asperger Publishing Co.

Garfinkle, A., and I. Schwartz. 2002. Peer imitation: Increasing social interactions in children with autism and other developmental disabilities in inclusive preschool classrooms. *Topics in Early Childhood Special Education* 22: 26-28.

Gassner, D. 2009. The third annual women's panel: Redefining success and strategies for achieving. Presented at Autism Society of America Conference, St. Charles, IL.

Goodwin, M., J. Groden, W. Velicer, L. Lipsitt, G. Baron, S. Hofmann, and G. Groden. 2006. Cardiovascular arousal in individuals with autism. *Focus on Autism and Other Developmental Disabilities* 21 (2): 100-123.

Grandin, T. 2006. *Animals in Translation.* New York: Simon and Schuster.

Grandin, T. 1996. Interview with Dr. Temple Grandin. *For individuals living with autism.* http://www.autism.com/ind_temple_interview.asp.

Grandin, T. 2008. Keynote address presented at the Autism Society of America Conference, Orlando, FL.

Grandin, T. 2002. Teaching tips for children and adults with autism. *For individuals living with autism.* http://www.autism.com/ind_teaching_tips.asp.

Grandin, T. 1995. *Thinking in Pictures: And other reports from my life with autism.* New York: Doubleday.

Grandin, T., and S. Barron. 2005. *Unwritten Rules of Social Relationships: Decoding social mysteries through the unique perspectives of autism.* Arlington, TX: Future Horizons.

Grandin, T., and K. Duffy. 2004. *Developing Talents: Careers for individuals with asperger syndrome and high-fuctioning autism.* Shawnee Mission, KS: Autism Asperger Publishing Co.

Grandin, T., and M. Scariano. 1986. *Emergence: Labeled autistic.* Novato, CA: Arena Press.

Gray, C. 1994. *Comic Strip Conversations.* Arlington, TX: Future Horizons.

Gray, C. 2000. *The New Social Story Book: Illustrated edition.* Arlington, TX: Future Horizons.

Gray, C. 2010. *The New Social Story Book, Revised and Expanded 10th Anniversary Edition: Over 150 social stories that teach everyday social skills to children with autism or asperger's syndrome, and their peers.* Arlington, TX: Future Horizons.

Groden, J., P. LeVasseur, A. Diller, and J. Cautela. 2002. *Coping with Stress Through PICTURE REHEARSAL: A how-to manual for working with individuals with autism and developmental disabilities.* Providence: The Groden Center.

Hale, M., and C. Hale. 1999. *I Had No Means to Shout!* Bloomington: 1st Books Library.

Hallahan, P., and J. Kauffman. 1993. *Exceptional Children: introduction to special education.* Boston: Allyn and Bacon

Hane, R. E., and V. Paradiz. 2009. Accepting and valuing difference. *Autism Advocate* 54 (1).

Haring, T., C. Breen, J. Weiner, C. Kennedy, and F. Bednersh. 1995. Using videotape modeling to facilitate generalized purchasing skills. *Journal of Behavioral Education* 5: 29-53.

Hill, D. A., and M. R. Leary. 1993. *Movement Disturbance: A clue to hidden competencies in persons diagnosed with autism and other development disabilities.* Madison: DRI Press.

Hodgdon, L. A. 1996. Visual Strategies for Improving Communication. Troy, MI: QuirkRoberts Publishing.

Hodgdon, L. A. 1999. Solving Behavior Problems in Autism: Improving communication with visual strategies. Troy, Michigan: QuirkRoberts Publishing.

Hollander, E. 2007. Living with autism in a world made for other. Health. CNN, February 22. http://www.cnn.com/2007/HEALTH/02/21/autism.amanda/index.html.

Hudson, J., and B. Myles. 2007. *Starting Points: The basics of understanding and supporting children and youth with asperger syndrome.* Shawnee Mission, KS: Autism Asperger Publishing Co.

Kanner, Leo. 1943. Autistic disturbances of affective contact. *NERV Child* 2: 217-50.

King, B. H. 2003. Preliminary studies of the use of digital video sampling to assess treatment response in children with autism. Grants funded by cure autism now 2003. http://www.autismspeaks.org/science/research/grants/funded_2003_can.php.

Kluth, P. 2005. Supporting students with autism: 10 ideas for inclusive classrooms. http://www.paulakluth.com/articles/tenideas.html.

Kluth, P. 2003. *You're Going to Love This Kid!: Teaching students with autism in the inclusive classroom.* Baltimore: Brookes Publishing Co.

Kluth, P., and P. Schwarz. 2008. *Just Give Him The Whale!: 20 ways to use fascinations, areas of expertise, and strengths to support students with autism.* Baltimore: Brookes Publishing Co.

Kluth, P., and J. Shouse. 2009. *The Autism Checklist: A practical reference for parents and teachers.* San Francisco: Jossey-Bass.

Kranowitz, C. 1998. *The Out-of-Sync Child.* New York: Berkley Publishing Group.

Kranowitz, C. 2003. *The Out of Sync Child Has Fun.* New York: Berkley Publishing Group

Lawson, W. 1998. *Life Behind Glass.* London: Jessica Kingsley Publishers.

Lovett, H. 1996. *Learning to Listen: Positive approaches and people with difficult behavior.* Baltimore: Brookes Publishing Co.

MADSEC (Maine Administrators of Services for Children with Disabilities). 2000. Report of the MADSEC autism task force. http://www.madsec.org.

Maple, S. 2008. Autistic girl kicked out of girl scout troop. *Parentdish,* Nov. 29. http://www.parentdish.com/2008/11/29/autistic-girl-kicked-out-of-girl-scout-troop/.

Maxwell, G., and J. Pringle. 1983. The analysis of video records. In *Using Video,* eds. P. Dowrick and S. Biggs, 61-71. New York: Wiley and Sons.

McCarthy, J. 2007. *Louder than Words: A mother's journey in healing autism.* New York: Dutton.

McGinnity, K., and N. Negri. 2005. *Walk Awhile in My Autism: A manual of sensitivity presentations to promote understanding of people on the autism spectrum.* Cambridge, WI: CBR Press.

McDonnell, J. 1993. *News from the Border: a mother's memoir of her autistic son.* New York: Houghton Mifflin.

McKean, T. A. 1994. *Soon Will Come the Light: A view from inside the autism puzzle.* Arlington, TX: Future Horizons.

Minshew, N. J., J. A. Sweeney, and M. L. Bauman. 1997. Neurological aspects of autism. In *Handbook of Autism and Pervasive Developmental Disorders,* eds. D. J. Cohen and A. Donnellan, 710-717. New York: Wiley and Sons.

Mukhopadhyay, T. R. 2000. *Beyond the Silence.* London: National Autistic Society.

Muzekari, L., and E. Kamis. 1973. The effects of videotape feedback and modeling on the behavior of chronic schizophrenics. *Journal of Clinical Psychology* 29: 313-316.

Myles, B. S., M. L. Trautman, and R. L. Schelvan. 2004. *The Hidden Curriculum: Practical so-*

lutions for understanding unstated rules in social situations. Shawnee Mission, KS: Autism Asperger Publishing Co.

Nash, J. M., and A. Bonesteel. 2002. The geek syndrome. *Time* 159 (18): 50-51.

Neumann, L. 2004. *Video Modeling: A visual teaching method for children with autism.* Croton, MD: Willerik Publishing.

Newport, J. 1999. Keynote address. ASW conference. http://www.asw4autism.org.

Newport, J., M. Newport, and J. Dodd. 2007. *Mozart and the Whale.* New York: Touchstone.

Newport, J., M. Newport. 2002. *Autism-Asperger's & Sexuality: Puberty and beyond.* Arlington, TX: Future Horizons, Inc.

Nikopoulos, C., and M. Keenan. 2003. Promoting social initiation in children with autism. *Behavioral Interventions* 18 (2): 87-108.

Nikopoulos, C., and M. Keenan. 2004a. Effects of video modeling on social interactions by children with autism. *Journal of Applied Behavior Analysis* 37: 93-96.

Nikopoulos, C., and M. Keenan. 2004b. Effects of video modeling on training and generalization of social initiation and reciprocal play by children with autism. *European Journal of Behavior Analysis* 5: 1-13.

Nikopoulos, C., and M. Keenan, M. 2006. *Video Modelling and Behaviour Analysis: A guide for Teaching Social Skills to Children with Autism.* London: Jessica Kingsley Publishers.

Notbohm, Ellen. 2005. *Ten Things Every Child with Autism Wishes You Knew.* Arlington, TX: Future Horizons, Inc.

Notbohm, Ellen. 2006. *Ten Things Your Student with Autism Wishes You Knew.* Arlington, TX: Future Horizons, Inc.

Patterson, J. 2002. *Movement Differences: data collected from first-hand accounts of autism.* University of San Diego. Unpublished.

Pitonyak, D. 2009. Workshop: Upside Down and Inside Out: supporting a person in crisis/supporting the people who care. Web: dimagine.com.

Prizant, B. M., A. M. Wetherby, E. Rubin, A. C. Laurat, and P. Rydell. 2006. *The SCERTS Model: Volume 1:* Assessment. Baltimore: Brookes Publishing.

Prizant, B.M., A. M. Wetherby, E. Rubin, A. C. Laurat, and P. Rydell, P. 2006. *The SCERTS Model: Volume II:* Program Planning and Intervention. Baltimore: Brookes Publishing.

Robledo, J., and A. Donnellan. 2008. Properties of supportive relationships from the perspective of academically successful individuals with autism. *Intellectual and Developmental Disabilities* 46 (4): 299-310.

Ross, A. 1981. *Child Behavior Therapy: Principles, procedures, and empirical basis.* New York: Wiley and Sons.

Sacks, O. 1995. *An Anthropologist on Mars: Seven paradoxical tales.* New York: Knopf.

Schopler, E., and G. Mesibov, eds. 1992. *High-Functioning Individuals with Autism.* New York: Plenum Press.

Schreibman, L., C. Whalen, and A. Stahmer. 2000. The use of video priming to reduce disruptive transition behavior in children with autism. *Journal of Positive Behavioral Interventions* 2: 3-11.

Schunk, D., and A. Hanson. 1989. Self-modeling and children's cognitive skill learning. *Journal of Educational Psychology* 81: 155-63.

Sherer, M., K. Pierce, S. Paredes, K. Kisacky, B. Ingersoll, and L. Schreibman. 2001. Enhancing conversational skills in children with autism via video technology. Which is better, "self" or "other" as a model? *Behavior Modification* 25: 140-158.

Shipley-Benamou, R., J. Lutzker, and M. Taubman. 2002. Teaching daily living skills to children with autism through instructional video modeling. *Journal of Positive Behavior Interventions* 4: 165-175.

Shore, S. 2003. *Beyond the Wall: Personal experiences with autism and asperger syndrome.* Second ed. Shawnee Mission, KS: Autism Asperger Publishing Co.

Strandt-Conroy, K. 1999. *Exploring movement differences in autism through first-hand accounts.* Dissertation, University of Wisconsin-Madison.

Summerfield, A. 1983. Recording social interaction. In *Using Video,* eds. P. Dowrick and S. Biggs, 61-71. New York: Wiley and Sons.

Tammet, D. 2006. *Born on a Blue Day: Inside the Extraordinary Mind of an Autistic Savant.* New York: Free Press.

Taylor, B., L. Levin, and S. Jasper. 1999. Increasing play-related statements in children with autism toward their siblings: Effects of video modeling. *Journal of Developmental Disabilities* 11: 253-264.

Television, video highly effective teaching tool for elementary to high school students—National Teacher Training Institute, 2003. Web. Special-kids.com.

Udvari-Solner, A., and P. Kluth. 2008. *Joyful Learning: Active and Collaborative Learning in Inclusive Classrooms.* Thousand Oaks, CA: Corwin Press.

Wallis, C. 2006. Inside the autistic mind. *Time* 167 (20): 43-51.

Wert, B., and J. Neisworth. 2003. Effects of video self-modeling on spontaneous requesting in children with autism. *Journal of Positive Behavior Interventions* 5: 300-305.

Wenig, M. 2003. *YogaKids: Educating the whole child through yoga.* New York: Harry N. Abrams.

Williams, D. L., G. Goldstein, and N. Minshew. 2006. The profile of memory function in children with autism. *Neuropsychology* 20 (1): 21-29.

Williams, D. 1992. *Nobody Nowhere.* New York: Times Books.

Williams, D. 1994. *Somebody Somewhere.* New York: Times Books.

Williams, D. 1996a. *Like Color to the Blind.* New York: Times Books.

Williams, D. 1996b. *Autism: An inside-out approach.* Philadelphia: Jessica Kingsley Publishers.

Williams, D. 1998. *Autism and Sensing: The unlost instinct.* Philadelphia, PA.: Jessica Kingsley Publishers.

Williams, M. S., and S. Shellenberger. 1994. *How Does Your Engine Run?: A leader's guide to the alert program for self-regulation.* Albuquerque: Therapy Works, Inc.

Williams, S. 2009. The culture of autism. Presented at Autism Society of America Conference, St. Charles, IL.

Wright, C., and D. Smith. 2009. The effect of PETTLEP on strength performance. *International Journal of Sport Exercise Psychology* 7 (1): 18-31.

Young, S. 2010. *Real People, Regular Lives: Autism, communication and quality of live.* http://www.iodbookstore.org/products/Real-People%2C-Regular-Lives.html.

Young, S. 2000. *Sensory and Movement Differences in Autism.* Unpublished manuscript.

APPENDIX I

Photo/Video Authorization and Release

I, ______________________, of ______________________ authorize ______________________ (the 'Photographer'), to use:

1. film photographs
2. digital photographs
3. motion picture footage
4. audio recordings

of ______________________ in accordance with the following terms:

Theme of Materials The Materials will be recorded and used with the understanding that the content or theme thereof will be the following: __________

____

____

Location The Materials will be recorded at or around the following location(s):

____

Schedule The approximate time during which the Materials will be recorded is: ____

Reproduction and Use: ____

____

Dated: ____

Signed: ____

APPENDIX II

Sample Social Script: Working in a Group (Academics)

Communication Function	Possible Messages
Attention Getter	*Hey guys*
Starter	*Let's figure out who is going to do what for the group.*
Continuations/Turn Shifts	*I can do research if you guys want.* *What do you want to do?* *That sounds good.* *Do we have everything?*
Closing	*I think we are all set.* *We can talk again next class.*

Storyboard

Name(s): ____________ Date: ____________ Period: ____________

1

2

3

4

5

6

Storyboard

Name(s): ____________________ Date: ____________ Period: ________

1

Jeffrey is done with class after 8th hour. He exits the room.

2

Jeffrey stops at his locker

3

Jeffrey gets his backpack on and walks toward the bus.

4

Jeffrey exits the school.

5

Jeffrey walks to bus number 68.

6

Jeffrey gets on the bus and goes home.